We Found Peace

We Found Peace

by GRAY CAMPBELL

THOMAS ALLEN LIMITED
TORONTO

To

THE SILENT PARTNERS

AND

OUR ENTHUSIASTIC FRIENDS

WITH GRATITUDE AND AFFECTION

Chapter One

EVERYONE thought we were quite mad in 1946. It just didn't make sense. I can understand now the lack of sympathy among friends and relatives in Eastern Canada, their pity for the young girl of twenty-two whom I had married in war-torn England during 1941 and for the child she had borne. They did not care how I wasted my life. But why should I be selfish enough to drag Eleanor and three year old Dane into a doubtful future of struggle and obviously bitter disappointment? The crazy uncertainty of it all! Hadn't my wife enough sense and control over my restlessness to ensure her own security and future happiness?

We were then in Hamilton, Ontario, making last minute plans to trek West in our modern covered wagon. Eleanor, morally convinced that her mission in life was to discover where I could fit into the scheme of things, was daily becoming alive to the promise of adventure. There must be a place, a condition of living somewhere, that would untangle the jittery nerves and the lost feeling of post-war uncertainty. In spite of pleadings and dire forecasts we were cutting our ties, quitting the job with a glowing future,

1

and driving west in a 1939 Ford pulling a second-hand trailer, to start again.

How could those who had not shared the war years interpret our mood? Ours was a war-time marriage. There wasn't a thing to recommend its future to a discriminating parent. Eleanor's mother and father, bless them, saw only one logical reason for the union. Their daughter was happy in her first love. And her mother got her teeth into the idea. For better or for worse, however bad it might be, and certainly she had no reason for great hopes, her lovely daughter should not rebound to a second choice. She had faced this fact with blind instinct even when, in discussing such a vague future as we faced, reason intruded through the fleeting, blissful days of courtship that were allowed us.

The war years—the wasted years, you say. I wonder. By the grace of God a lot of people matured during that time. It separated the men from the boys. Those who experienced it from the fringe of effort, can they possibly imagine how it was to be caught up in the vortex and to have one's sense of values and feeling for life change out of recognition? Everyone comes to a point where he asks himself, What do I want out of life? When we married in June of 1941 we simply wanted a chance to live together, with a desperate, hurried feeling that we were not to be cheated out of whatever marriage had to offer, in spite of war. There was no time to consider the future. You couldn't see farther than the next few days or weeks. A leave that could be figured in hours, a haven of peace away from the bombing, a period of flying to the next leave. That was it. You could reason it to stretch on as long as mind and coordination of instinct and body for self-preservation could manage the miracle of keeping alive.

Someone, somewhere, made the point that war is nothing more nor less than a concentrated dose of life. That is stripping away a lot of unnecessary verbiage. Fine then, let's get everything we are entitled to. You fancy yourself living on borrowed time, too impatient for your share to think of the rest.

During 1941 I was flying "bits of wood and cardboard tenuously supporting twin engines, held together by cold water paste and glue", as one technical officer put it, at the R.A.F. College. While the cream of the class went on to Hampdens, Whitleys and Beaufighters, I remained behind on the staff to instruct, serving in the same flight where I had spent anxious weeks as a pupil. "Plenty of time to get on ops," the Flight Commander said. "The war won't end next week and we'll all get a crack at it." I realized the truth of this in 1944, starting a tour on Lancasters, when next I saw this nerveless, considerate Englishman, Wing Commander John F. Sutton, D.S.O., D.F.C., A.F.C. If memory serves me right he picked up these decorations in a record eleven months about the time Guy Gibson was making his trips to Buck House.

Such memories remain green. And they cannot be denied expression although they compel me to wander pleasantly from the main story. Their account may read like deliberate procrastination and my writer's conscience imagines an impatient reader muttering: "Get along with it, boy. All this is by the way." But is it? Could there be a spark of hope or faith in these wanderings enough to console some youth in

3

these troubled times? To understand more completely the forces that combined to direct our path to our own idea of the full life, from troubled waters to calm, the reader must follow or endure the digressions. As a doctor digs into a patient's past for clues to a difficult diagnosis, so must we cover the war's bearing on our subsequent actions and perhaps subconsciously uncover evidence to satisfy the discriminating mind of the interested reader. Recently a paragraph in Joseph Conrad's writing caught my attention. Pleading in 'A Personal Record' that "the public record of these formative impressions is not the whim of an uneasy egotism", he goes on to say: "Only in men's imagination does every truth find an effective and undeniable existence. Imagination, not invention, is the supreme master of art as of life. An imaginative and exact rendering of authentic memories may serve worthily that spirit of piety towards all things human which sanctions the conceptions of a writer of tales, and the emotions of the man reviewing his own experience."

You may want to know what was behind the person in Air Force uniform. There was very little of interest to fill out the character. He imagined himself important in the eyes of his contemporaries, who were all English. But in truth he was just another undistinguished Canadian with no more background than any stereotyped character—a spotty education, no deep roots, countless friends and seven careless years in the Royal Canadian Mounted Police, beginning at the age of twenty. It is necessary to point this out because the police years afforded service in the West, in the Alberta short grass, foothill and mountain country.

4

So he was twenty-seven when the war started. But he had not grown up. He was an untested boy scout. The formative years were ahead. The war years.

The good people in England were wonderfully kind to, and tolerant of, the mad but dedicated crowd who arrived in England during September of 1939. About sixty of us found ourselves at Uxbridge in the Royal Air Force with the lowly rank of Aircraftsman, Second Class, at two shillings a day. On our bed cards in the barracks we had stubbornly printed our trade as 'Pilot', and you can well imagine what reaction this cheek set up among the drill corporals who looked after us. They figured out some wonderful jobs for the 'pilots' I can assure you. A depressing start when one considers that they had travelled to England from all parts of the globe at their own expense, offering their services— and their lives. They had converged from South Africa, Canada, Australia, New Zealand, even from Hong Kong. They were young, but they had high standards and they matured rapidly. They were not an easy bunch to control or discipline until they got into the air. At the end only a handful of the gay crew were still around, but they left their names and their transient fame in many places.

Bill Deas was from South Africa, a long, lean Gary Cooper type. His uncle was a General—the name sounded like van der Spey—on the military staff at South Africa House. Bill had a fantastic hatred of the Nazis and an almost over- whelming impatience to get a crack at the enemy. It never wore off. He was a class ahead of me at Cranwell and went on to Hampdens for his first tour. Legend had it that Bill refused the usual instructing period of rest between tours

5

and much of the leave due him. Toward the end of the Cranwell course we had our last short leave together. I still have the pen he gave me then. We were travelling to Purley, in Surrey, and were leaving London by train when one of the early fire blitzes started. Bill was shocked and deeply enraged by the savage attack. That night from our bedroom window we watched London burn and were the only ones in the household to sleep above ground. Such was our ignorance of this side of the war. A house on the next street was destroyed and two children died inside from escaping gas. I am sure Bill always remembered that night.

Returning to our station on Sunday we were coming in to London during a lull when the sirens went again. On our way to King's Cross Station all hell broke loose. We felt restless in the crowded station, waiting for a train that might not start, and made our way across the street to a pub whose imperfect black-out showed it to be still open. While everyone else hurried underground Bill pushed open the door and strode in. Alone, I might have followed the crowds to shelter. But from the night before Bill had on his mind the memory of London burning, and he was resentful. We cheered up to find that the pub had been taken over by the Navy, a group of very salty tars, mostly middle-aged, regulars all. The Navy cheered the Air Force. It was obvious they had taken a crack at the enemy and were about to rejoin their ship. They were all balancing pints and gave us a hearty welcome. Concussion from some near misses blew the black-out around but the Navy took no notice whatever of any intrusion on their last night ashore. I could not hold myself in any longer and made tentative enquiry about the

6

extent of this raid. One old hand cocked an ear, deigned to take notice and said: "Sounds like 'itler is getting narsty about somefink, matey," before getting on with the business of drinking and enjoying himself. Later when miraculously the train pulled out, we spotted the merry crew of sailors making it at the last possible minute.

I saw Bill once more, and heard of his exploits later. He picked up a lot of decorations. Then toward the end of the war one of the early types visited our squadron. Any news of Bill Deas? "Good old Bill," he said. "He was commanding a four-engine squadron not many weeks ago. On his third tour of ops and crowding seventy trips when he bought it. But don't feel too badly about Bill. He had a good innings and would be the first to admit it."

And then there was Pat, from Johannesburg. Before he became a fighter boy at Malta we knew him as a quiet-spoken, serious chap who had been a medical student. But he had an Irish temper and a saving Irish sense of humour. At home he was famous as a distance runner, a miler. From Uxbridge we had been sent to the coast where in resort hotels from Hastings to St. Leonards-on-Sea thousands of embryo aircrew were billeted. Pat loved to work off energy at a prohibitive hour by clipping along the water front. As he passed each hotel he would pick up the challenge of Service Police who wanted to know what the airman was doing on the streets. They would clatter after Pat, who wasn't showing any turn of speed, and would be led by the other hotels until he had picked up a respectable following of police trying to run him down. Then Pat would swing off the sea front to the hilly section in order to test their

7

condition. If they lagged he would slow down and the field would renew their efforts. After getting himself nicely warmed up and the pack well strung out, Pat would sprint out of sight, double back via an alley to our hotel and climb the water pipes and roofs to his room. "Man, that was fun," he would say.

About November, 1939, South Africa House in London decided to do something for their boys. A cocktail party and dance was laid on and these good Joes decided to make me an honorary South African for the occasion. We had a great time tasting this luxury away from the stagnation and greasy boredom of AC2's on a holding unit. The day after the party we were assembled before a very keen and smart Inspector from Scotland Yard who wanted to know the circumstances surrounding the sudden death of one of our number. The poor chap had fallen out of a window in a hotel off Piccadilly during the darkest of black-outs. Pat was the last to appear in the round-up but he had the best story to tell of his experiences the night before. We had been shaken by the tragedy and needed diversion. Seated in a cozy saloon bar that afternoon, Pat told us the following yarn.

"You chaps probably won't believe this, but after the dance I wandered off by myself. I found some obscure little drinking clubs and vague companions who seemed to be good pals while the money lasted. Pretty soon I wasn't feeling any pain and drifted off by myself. The rest is second-hand because I don't remember. But around four or five Sunday morning apparently I am wandering through the dim, deserted streets of London not knowing where I

8

am going, and not caring much. I have lost my service cap and respirator. This catches the eye of a lonely Bobby. The copper wants to know my name and where I'm staying. I'm not much help. Then he notices 'South Africa' on my shoulder patch and this probably arouses pity. Anyway he is about to go off duty and decides to take me along.

"I don't remember a thing, but the big fellow hauls me to his flat, gets his good wife to change her place in bed for the sofa in the bedroom. He undresses me, puts me in his wife's place, then dosses down himself. About ten o'clock I open an eye and try to figure out where I am. Across the room I spot the woman asleep and turning over I notice this big hulking man in bed with me. I jump smartly out of bed without a stitch on, slap the fellow across the buttocks, strike a fighting attitude and yell: 'What the hell are *you* doing here?'

"The copper's wife begins to laugh. He rolls over and gently tells me to get back in bed and cover up. I do this and he proceeds to give me the grift. They were fine people. The Bobby says: 'Mother, this boy needs attention. You'd better fix up some breakfast.' Afterwards we drift down to a pub and have a good laugh."

Such were the men who made up our tight little crowd. We shared our luck, good and bad. But we drifted quickly and completely apart when we started flying, catching odd glimpses of each other momentarily in London or at remote airfields.

At the very end of the war I spotted a familiar figure for a few seconds in the Haymarket but couldn't stop the bus I was on. It was Spug Whiting, and he was limping. I set

9

out to check the town—not too difficult a task because we invariably travelled in a small orbit. Later that day when our paths crossed at the Brevet Club I learned he had been flying Spitfires around Sumatra, had also drifted up Iran way. He had a bad foot and a piece of cannon shell still in his chest. He had suffered dengue fever and dysentery but had changed little otherwise. At least he was still alive, and as we added up the score we knew we both had beaten the odds against us. He tried to scare me. "Listen to what I'm telling you, chum. I ran into those Russians. We used the same airfield. Those babies are spoiling for trouble. I never saw anything so cocky or stupid. Mark my words, we'll be fighting those b - - - - - - s in another five years." That was in 1945.

Let's go back to 1939 for a moment. From early in the war Lady Frances Ryder in London was doing an enormous job helping to keep us out of mischief. She had some grand people helping her entertain and her house was always open to welcome the strangers from across the seas. Officials in our legations would suggest we drift around there to take tea. Our own L. B. Pearson at Canada House gave us the word and on one occasion Lady Frances interviewed me. I am afraid we were rather trying cases at the time, bitter about hanging around as AC2's—trade 'Pilot'. She arranged several charming invitations and on my return to the dreary station I received letters asking me to week-ends at country homes in Yorkshire.

Not until I had graduated from Cranwell did I accept. It was a fateful day when I journeyed to Robin Hood's Bay. For there I met Eleanor. In spite of the war, in spite of the fact I was crowding twenty-nine and thought I was safe—this was it! Tall, graceful, athletic and accomplished, she brought fun to everything we did together, from walking in the rain to sipping tea before the coziest of fires. It was wonderful, but frightening because of the war. I wanted to sneak out and send myself a wire recalling to duty. But I was weak and stayed on. I talked to Eleanor about Canada and the days of peace. I tried to express my nostalgic memories of the happy days in Alberta. Like all people in love among new friends and kindly strangers we were confident that no one knew our secret. But to Mr. and Mrs. Harold Shepherd, our hosts, it must have been quite obvious.

Back at the College the foulest of winter weather washed out flying and I wrote letters to Eleanor for ten days. Nothing seemed quite the same. I sneaked back to Yorkshire for a week-end, met her at Leith Rigg, then at the home of Leo Walmsley, the Yorkshire author. We became engaged. On the next leave I journeyed to her home to meet her mother, buying the ring first. We were engaged for three months but it seemed like an eternity.

It was a real war-time marriage, but neither the vicar nor anyone else threw it at us. We were together two months, then separated for seven. I faced the choice of being posted to Kenya to instruct or going back to Canada. I couldn't take my wife to Kenya. I couldn't get her to Canada either, but we didn't know that and after running into sticky red tape I had a stroke of good luck. While flying a kite from Halifax to Calgary I ran into Mr. L. B. Pearson at the Chateau Laurier cafeteria. When I told him the British

11

were holding up Eleanor's passport he agreed that she was now a Canadian and managed to reunite the Campbell family.

After parting for seven months we lived together for a short time in Calgary. Then the station moved to Swift Current where we spent a year and we began collecting furniture for after the war. For the first time since our marriage life had an even tenor. We began to have faith in the future. Dane was born at Swift Current in 1943 and we had the world by the tail. It was too good to last. There was a sudden posting back to England. The station broke up. Eleanor sold everything we had accumulated, packed and stored a few personal things and moved to Calgary to visit friends. I wangled leave from New Brunswick, flew back to Calgary but failed to see her settled. She managed to rent a one-room summer cottage just outside the city, hung on until the snow drove her out, then travelled East to Ottawa with baby and dog to stay with my sister. The personal treasures and the wedding gifts we had never opened were left stored in Calgary. Some day we hoped to be back.

This second period in England was joyless. Whereas the others were returning to families and friends, I seemed to be more astray than the first time. The original crowd had scattered far and wide. Then I joined the squadron. They were flying Lancs and had a wizard Wing Commander, Sellick, on his third tour. Sellick only put his name on the battle order for the stickiest targets, and when the crews saw it there most of them had ring trouble. He was a right guy and everyone worshipped him with reason.

12

It was a tails-up squadron, 576. About a third of the boys were Canucks. A few of us were married types with our wives at home. There was a certain security to life at the squadron. You had thirty-two trips to make. Okay, let's get it over. Get as many trips in as quickly as possible. Kiel, Hamburg, Cologne, Stuttgart, Leipsig, Bochum. Come on, Johnny, put me down for tonight, I'll find a spare gunner. Life on the squadron changed a lot of things. Sometimes life was grim; it was war and it was for keeps. A lot of the best crews simply disappeared. Sometimes there was fragmentary evidence. We picked our buddies carefully, tried not to get too friendly. It wasn't like the early days. If you relaxed you went large on the right rein. You couldn't stop to speculate or dream. Maybe you let yourself go in letters, but you wouldn't admit it. You hesitated to get too close with anyone but your own crew. Close friends had a nasty habit of leaving a big gap. And you treated replacement crews like outcasts.

I remember a new skipper arriving with his bunch to replace one of the best crews we had ever had. You hated to look his way because he reminded you of the loss and made you wonder just what had happened. It wasn't the poor guy's fault, but for weeks he was left outside the pale. Johnny Acheson spoke to him first and said to me: "Cam, this fellow is O.K." So we cultivated him, and indeed he was. We began to forget the other crew. When the skipper got word his wife had been delivered of a son we all helped him celebrate. We began to look for him in the mess, share

13

our jokes and horseplay. Against our better judgment we accepted him.

Not many nights later we returned from a hot target. Johnny and I waited in the briefing room until about two in the morning. But he didn't show, and the Intelligence Officer sent us to bed. We couldn't sleep. Next morning we heard he had sent a signal from the channel—on fire, one member of the crew dead, trying to make Manston, an emergency field in the south. Just as he was limping in on final approach his kite fell apart.

They picked up enough remnants for seven coffins and had a big funeral down south. No one from the squadron was present but most of the relatives were, and we thought of the young skipper's widow with the baby. Back at the squadron we withdrew into our shells.

Some weeks later Johnny came into my room. "Remember the swell crew that got it at Manston, Cam? Listen to this. The rear gunner was married as well. Just the other day he walks into his home. His wife must have thought she was seeing a ghost. She had buried him with the rest, saw the coffin lowered with his name on it. He says the skipper gave them a chance to bail out over France, and he had. Doesn't know if anyone else did. The gunner beat his way back, didn't report anywhere until he saw his wife. Imagine the flap at the Air Ministry, re-rigging the records. It makes you wonder if any others got out, but I guess the skipper is a write-off."

There was a kid from London driving a transport that took crews out to their dispersals for a show and brought them back to Intelligence afterwards. We thought he was crazy because he would beg the skippers to take him along whenever the target was a big one in Germany. He managed to attend to his job somehow, being absent only during the operation. I suppose his buddies covered up for him. The skippers who took him said the lad went nuts over the target. He used to shovel out pamphlets and generally help the bomb aimer. I refused to take him and talked him out of one trip when the crew he had arranged to fly with went missing. It made me curious. I could understand his wanting to make one trip, but not night after night. Then I was told he had lost his entire family when his home was hit in a blitz.

After you had chalked up twenty trips and could see the end of the tour you might allow yourself to think vaguely of home. What would it be like? Would we pick up where we had left off? Could it ever be the same again? No one could find the answer. Toward the end, too, we had a wistful desire to keep on sticking together, we boys from Canada. But we didn't know that forces beyond our control would decree otherwise. We didn't even come home on the same ship after leaving the squadron, although we finished duty within days of each other. I think most of us were lost souls. We had left some part of ourselves behind in England. It was hard to talk or associate with anyone not from the squadron. It was difficult to think about anyone but the crews of those Lancasters . . . and the incidents. Remember the flak over Cologne, and the daylight job when Dixie stopped a piece of shrapnel? Boy, that Bochum was hot! A concentrated dose of life. And the largest dose was the squadron.

15

Eleanor met me in Montreal. We had a shake-down cruise around the restaurants and night clubs. Dane was waiting in Ottawa, and Eleanor, in her great wisdom, had taken a cottage at a friendly lake for a month. In spite of careful briefing Dane was strange and shy with his father. But with Eleanor's wonderful cooking, fishing expeditions and games to excite a little boy, in no time he was calling me 'Daddy', and a new life opened for us both. It was pure magic, but like all good illusions it couldn't last. I began to worry about a job, a place to live. The plans we had made in 1941 seemed very remote.

Chapter Two

AFTER six years and better in the Royal Air Force how does one settle down? Can a person throw off the uniform, change to a suit of civvies, mix with the crowds and just forget? By putting away log books with several thousand hours of flying, can one erase the memories of those exciting years? There was the grim forced landing on a hill top in England. Shouldn't have walked away from that one, coming down through fog to four hundred feet. The trips over Germany entered in red ink, each laconic line opening the flood-gates of the mind to a story that still grips the innards. The times we went to Cologne and always picked up flak. We thought we had had it over Bochum. But we came through. Could we pick up the old life right where we had left off?

The home town seemed incredibly tiny and strange. Only Pappy, a navigator from the old squadron, was around. We were together as much as possible to swap yarns, always talking about the crews. The present seemed unreal; the past made sense. It was hard to mix with others or make friends with strangers who hadn't been there. Perhaps if I had returned to the R.C.M.P. the old uniform and routine

17

might have been a fair exchange. With luck it might have taken us back to Alberta. But Eleanor had experienced enough of service life. We wanted a life of our own. And I had to prove to her, to the friends and relatives back in England, that she had married well. The offer of a position in a local firm had wonderful opportunities. The fact that I had no previous business experience did not seem to be a prohibiting factor. They would train me. It was a fine organization with a young outlook and a happy family atmosphere among employees.

Months of tuition followed at the factory, absorbing the business, studying at night, learning and practising and orienting. We rented a converted chicken coop at the edge of the city, bought a second hand car and felt more bewildered in the strange environment. Eleanor spent her days on the outskirts with Dane while I was trying to pick up business methods in the city. Demonstrations, meetings, classes, days in the field with the trained men. Daily assurances that I was a bright boy destined to go on and up. Selling business systems.

When it was time to solo we were sent to Hamilton, Ontario. Here was the big opportunity for the right man, a tough competitive market. It seemed that all the industrial might of Canada was located there. But our first few months were plagued with finding a place to live. Had we been alone, just the two of us, it might have been easy. But we had Dane and a cocker spaniel. The dog wasn't such a problem but the child proved a terrible handicap. We paced the streets, advertised, chased all kinds of leads. Finally the Veterans' Administration sent us to a small hotel where we rented a single room over a beer parlour. The steady hum of voices below was soothing, but the smoke drifted upstairs through the rooms, hanging heavy like a London fog. It was difficult to sustain the buoyancy and optimism needed for the business of selling.

Finally in desperation we bought a trailer. Dane wouldn't have to be bottled up constantly and fed in restaurants. He was getting out of hand. We moved to a trailer camp and felt more independent. When we changed location to a summer cottage district by Lake Ontario where we could swim and play on the beach, Eleanor, Dane and the dog had their first break.

As their spirits rose, mine declined. Big business didn't show any interest in the new man. There were plenty of old timers who had been around for years. Some of the large factories were shut down with a wave of strikes, narrowing the field. In addition the chilling realization began to dawn that I never would be suited for the business. Perhaps we had two strikes against us because we were living in the past. We were not making enough new friends, and those we met were always being compared with the old ones, to their disadvantage. Chaps coming home from war would do well to remember this. Don't expect to find conditions as they were when you left. Nothing seems quite the same, but it isn't the old home town that has changed—it is you. When you get back on your own you have to stand up and walk again. Seldom is it easy and it doesn't pay to try leaning on the buddies who shared the war years. Perhaps the whole question of success or failure in settling down depends upon a state of mind.

In our case when we tried to face our dilemma we were licked right at the start. I felt submerged in a crowded world of unfriendly strangers. One man who had kept the home fires burning cautioned me not to excuse my newness at the job by referring to the fact that I was otherwise occupied during the war years. "Around here," he said, "nobody cares."

From frustration I slid into a hopeless feeling of inferiority in everything I did. There seemed no escape and no point in struggling on. What could I do? What was I fitted for in this rat race? There was no answer. What would I like to do? Ah, that was better. I would like to fly again. But Eleanor did not approve. It would take a change of environment, a drastic change, to pull out of this slump. There was a subconscious yearning to return to the West, preferably Alberta. Perhaps I could recapture out there the old feeling of buoyancy that always sustained me through ups and downs during the seven years in the Police. How about returning to the R.C.M.P.? Eleanor was not too enthusiastic, but she was now ready to try anything that held a promise to restore the old spirit. So I wrote to the Commissioner. The Adjutant replied that they would offer me my old rank if I travelled with wife and family at my own expense to New Brunswick!

What were we struggling for, here and now, in Hamilton, Ontario? To make enough money in the next ten years so that we could live the way we wanted. It had always been our dream, from the first walk on the Yorkshire moors, to have a home in the country with horses to ride, dogs and children to train, to be able to live off the soil. But we had to have money.

We read a book entitled 'Ten Acres and Independence'. We read pamphlets put out by the government for establishing veterans on the soil. We had considered this government plan while I was still on the squadron and hoped to profit by it later after we had become established. With this in view we had not used our war service gratuity for immediate needs. It was still there if we could qualify. But could we transfer it to the West where we both wanted to live? It was a faint hope. At this stage I was not sleeping well, and when thinking through the night began to doubt myself capable of achieving the simplest plan. Always in the past after being slammed down for the count I had managed to bounce back on my feet. I remembered the bounces. But this time there was no fight left. Was I the sort of person who functions only in the mass, with a squadron behind him for moral support? Could I not navigate myself? Would I always need a crew?

One night Eleanor woke up when I was lighting a third cigarette and shook me out of lethargy. "Let's do something about it right now," she said. "We can't go on like this. Chuck the job and start again. I won't argue even if you go back to flying. Start working on the next move. And for goodness sake don't start feeling sorry for yourself. I can't stand self-pity."

Some flying schools were located between town and the trailer. I did a few hours in Cubs, obtaining a limited commercial license in Toronto. I also wrote to friends in Swift Current, Medicine Hat and Banff. Those wonderful Westerners threw the ball right back and left out the platitudes. They did not question our motives or offer negative advice. Every reply carried the warmth and expansiveness of the West together with the spirit that made it great.

From Swift Current Edgar Burke wrote that his son and

21

other young men were interested in a flying school. They had a license and were looking for an instructor. He figured I could fit in. There would be charter work besides. It didn't read like a letter from a retired business man for it carried the enthusiasm of a twenty-year-old.

Tip Volway wired us from Medicine Hat. About to leave for Toronto on business, he sent us time of arrival and a request to meet him at the station.

Pete and Catharine Whyte wrote from Banff. Why wait ten years to make enough money? Come out now before we all get that old. By the time you make enough money to do what you want it may be too late. They also sent R. H. Bennett's book, 'The Compleat Rancher', directed to veterans who might be casting around for an outdoor, active life.

Eleanor and I read that book, lived with it every waking moment, memorized sections that argued in our favour. Here was the answer, something concrete that crystallized our own vague longing for independence, for a permanent, lifelong pursuit in which we could be equal partners with a family. Raising and improving a herd of beef cattle, building a home from the land—for us, we felt, that was it. Though I still had trouble sleeping my mind was afire with ideas. If you get hold of a dream and chase it through hell and high water, you may not complete its realization in the original but you will have a lot of fun trying.

That was the decision we made. I also thought of the very real partnership in such a dream—Eleanor and I, and later the children, riding our own land, working our own cattle, taking off our own crops. Doing everything together. We didn't stop to think rationally or put down a bunch of figures on paper. That might scare us. A powerful urge took hold. We would not tolerate the arguments of logic. There wasn't time. We just had a feeling about it—a crazy, excited feeling that we were going to grab the world by the tail. And with our dream we compared our present condition carried to the ultimate—my days spent in offices and factories, Eleanor at home with the children, my return in the evenings too tired and dull to discuss anything that had happened during the day, living separate lives, growing farther apart. Was there any partnership in that? The sales manager had lectured me about joining clubs and organizations, cultivating business friends, living the business by day and night. It worked out that if you were making ten thousand a year you were expected to spend some eight thousand living up to the job—entertaining, joining, chasing. A hell of a life. On the other hand Mr. Bennett says on page . . .

So I resigned from the firm, to be effective the end of September, 1946. Tip arrived in Toronto and I drove him to the trailer on Lake Ontario. He had a shave, introduced us to a drink, reminisced about friends in the West, then got down to business. "When are you coming West? Sure you are. I talked over this flying business with the boys. No future in it. Now you two know the West. Your best bet is to start ranching. You are suited for it. Mack Higdon, Gene Burton, Harry Hargrave and the rest will give you lots of advice. Don't forget nearly all the old timers started from scratch and you don't want to expect any different treatment. You know all your friends will be pulling for you. Come straight to our house if you land in the Hat. Use it for your headquarters. Now I want to say something

23

to Eleanor and I don't want her to forget it. You have to be ready now, if things are slow starting to break for you, to see your husband in some hotel slinging beer or running a hamburger joint. But what the hell. The main thing is to get started, and if you are in that frame of mind you'll win. Are you game, Eleanor? I knew you would be. I'm just warning you, that's all."

Dear old Tip! He's gone now to another range. His passing is a great loss to Medicine Hat and countless friends throughout the country. Wherever he is you may be sure there is laughter and good fellowship. But memories are green in the West and a fellow like that lives on in the hearts of his friends.

Tip had given us the final shove. The die was cast. We hooked trailer to car, stocked up with food for the trip through the States and headed for the border with about eighty dollars in cash and a million dollars' worth of enthusiasm.

Chapter Three

As WE ROLLED along the highway, day after day, with our worldly belongings now pushing, now pulling and swaying behind the car in our little trailer, there was, for me, a definite feeling of suspension in time. Very unreal it was, as though we had stopped growing. Time stood still, and we were perched precariously between two periods in our life. The first day only brought a feeling of escape; succeeding days brought a sensation of no feeling at all. Behind us lay five years of war-time marriage—living in trunks, separations, travel, Leeds, London, Robin Hood's Bay, Lynmouth, Calgary, Swift Current. And like a bad dream the year of struggle on civvy street. Ahead lay only the vaguest image of the future we both wanted. We could not imagine the outcome. Its shape lay in our hands alone. But at the moment we had no choice of plan to accept or reject. We were not sure just where we would stop. In the meantime we were travelling in a vacuum. We could not pretend it was a holiday, not with the miles eating into our limited cash. We had nothing planned or set aside for emergency. No one knew when or how we were coming or where we might appear. The past was behind and we could not turn back.

Near Spread Eagle, Wisconsin, the car complained at the hills and we pulled into a remote cluster of cabins. The nearest garage was at the next town where we found a mechanic who accepted the risk of installing a new clutch for Canadian money. Here Eleanor managed to catch up with the washing while Dane and the dog let off some pent-up steam. I shuttled between our camp and the garage by bus, estimating probable cost and our dwindling food supply against the anxious pocket-book. Before disaster overtook us we managed to square away and get rolling again. The incident made us realize that we had a time factor to consider. Normal persons might have worried about the future but we felt that once we reached Alberta we would be home. It wasn't rational, but after the years of travel and uncertainty we were dead sure that as soon as we crossed into that province we should be safe. It was the same feeling I had after leaving a target and heading the Lancaster for England. The navigator only had to sing out: "Over the channel, Skip!" and when I could see the searchlights along the coast of England I would know with absolute certainty that another operation was safely behind.

But with the time factor narrowing our chances, would we get to Alberta? We were travelling the most northern route, avoiding the cities and enjoying the lakes and woods that afforded remote camping spots. When we hit the prairies our pace quickened and we began eating up the miles. At one lonesome spot we stopped before a huge sign that pointed north to Canada and, in large letters, SWIFT CURRENT. Was fate calling us this way? I turned to Eleanor and we recalled the kind, enthusiastic letter from Edgar Burke. Would we turn here to begin our adventure?

We remembered the friendly little city from 1942 when we were part of the R.A.F. Flying School that had moved there from Calgary. I was curious to investigate the flying set-up and talk things over with the Burkes. We remembered the other good citizens and also the fact there would be many missing faces. I rather favoured going that way. But Eleanor remarked that we both wanted to go ranching, that Alberta had been pulling us over the miles whereas it was only I who was interested in flying, and the idea did not seem down to earth compared to the glow we received just thinking of the promise in 'The Compleat Rancher'. We used to quote passages from the book to each other during the long spells of driving and were continually re-reading chapters. So I put the car in gear and drove on, not, I may say, without some doubt as we drew away from that promising turning point.

We seemed to be heading into strange country after that until we came to Havre, Montana. I had known this town during police days on border patrol, and as it was at the end of a long day of driving we decided to camp. Again we held council. Where would we go from here? I thought of Calgary, Lethbridge or Banff. Eleanor objected. "It doesn't make sense, going to a city or a mountain resort. We want to go ranching. If we head for those places you will invariably start visiting old friends to talk things over and you may get side-tracked into a city job."

"That's all very well," I argued, "but shouldn't we talk this over with government officials who run the Veterans' Land Act first?"

"That's the last thing we should do," she reasoned. "Can you picture getting a good reception when the nearest thing to ranching we have is a talking knowledge of this book? That would spoil everything. How about the big ranchers you used to know? Would they be interested in hiring a couple as green as we are, with a little boy as well? We are going to need experience before tackling the Veterans' Land Act. Mr. Bennett advises going as a working hand on a ranch, and if you think you have a lot to learn consider me and the problems I face for a moment."

I began to doubt the wisdom of setting out with an ideal but no plan. Was Tip's warning about to confront us and would I finish the long journey slinging beer in a hotel or slapping buns on hamburgers while looking for that break? The magic of green pastures that had pulled me out of a slump in Hamilton, the activity of getting ready, the anticipation of travelling had suddenly vanished here in Havre. We put Dane to bed in the trailer and walked along the main street. Nicely tanned cow men in big hats, jeans and riding boots were on the street, in hotels and driving large cars. They seemed like giants from the mysterious world of cow camps. We became excited again. I stopped one to ask if the old trail into Canada that took one to Medicine Hat was serviceable and still in use. "It's there all right, but with all the rain we've had I reckon you will need chains and lots of luck," he said.

Eleanor and I went into a hotel to sit down. I tried to think. Back in 1938 I had been stationed at Manyberries, real stock country. I had spent a memorable Christmas at the Bar N Bar ranch of Mack Higdon. Would Mack be there? I tried to remember the names of the cowboys. What would it be like arriving there, not as a member of the R.C.M.P. in the good old days but as another unsettled

28

veteran with no job or prospects and with a wife and child as well? I tried to recall other patrols, other ranches. By Jove, I had it! Between Manyberries and Havre was the Federal Government range experimental station. Yes, and Harry Hargrave had been in charge. Just the man to give some direction to our wanderings. Better still, Eleanor had met him in Swift Current when he attended the Saskatchewan Stock Growers' Convention there during the war.

"Do you remember Harry Hargrave, El?"

"You mean the nice chap who visited us one evening with Barney Crocket? Of course I do."

"Well, unless he's been moved his outfit is just north of this place—the Manyberries range experimental station. Would it make sense if we drove up that far tomorrow? I must warn you that I feel we should continue west to Coutts and enter Canada on the good road. It is hard surface and we could make Lethbridge tomorrow. You would have friends there while I looked around, but if you think we should go right for our target we could try this rough old trail to Harry's place."

"I think we should try to get to Harry's—you know how I feel about a city. Can we find out if he's still there?"

I tried the telephone and spoke to a man at the station. No, Harry was away but would return in a day or two. I gave my name and asked the chap to advise Harry I would be driving up from Havre to see him.

We started early and I found the trail by instinct. If Eleanor could get used to this, I thought, she would look at the other ranching districts as paradise. Mr. Bennett had described the foothills and mountain country, clear cool streams, cattle standing in lush, deep grass, evergreens and

29

warm chinook winds. We were driving along a rutted trail on sun-baked alkali flats. No trees, fences broken wherever they showed and, miles apart, the odd abandoned, broken-down dwelling. The centre of the trail was taken over by thick coils of rattlers and bull snakes. We drove over them with a bump and they didn't seem to notice.

Eleanor became alarmed. "Is this our country?" What grass cover there was seemed inadequate, a blade here, a blade there. No stock in sight. It was hot. I tried to tell her this was the famous short grass country of large ranches and big herds. She wasn't interested and perhaps I wasn't very convincing.

A stretch of mud appeared ahead with no sign of a detour. We tried to barge through. The trailer braked the car to a stop and the wheels began digging in. It was gumbo. Then the car boiled over. I began to think about the clutch and reconditioned motor. Up ahead we spotted another deserted house and barn. Perhaps I could find some water there. Eleanor decided to come along and we stepped gingerly, fearing snakes. I never could remember what month rattlers were dangerous. We found some water but shuddered at the sight of the buildings. Within fifty miles there seemed to be nothing alive but snakes and there was no reason to expect another car along this forsaken trail for a week. I guess it was desperation that got us out of the mud. Though I did not mention it I thought of turning back to Havre. But we continued, and after clearing Canadian Customs at Wild Horse, Alberta, we bumped and swayed until well in the afternoon when, like an oasis in the desert, we gazed at a belt of green trees. That must be the station. There would be people, water and possibly a reason for this stupid drive.

But when we arrived we found only strangers. Harry had not returned. We could camp near one of the houses and hook on to the lights. The little boy and the dog would be safe on the lawn but they had better watch out for snakes. The foreman would be along soon and if we required anything we could ask him. He lived in the nearest house. We went to bed that night wondering if this was just another camp stop or if we were close to the end of our journey. A lot would depend upon the interview next day.

In the morning I was out walking at six, trying to figure out a line of talk for Harry. A door slammed, and I turned to see a big fellow hurrying across the lawn in my direction. He sure looked familiar, and then I started to grin. It was Eddie Goodfellow. The big moose was miles from his own pasture. He used to run the bus and mail north of Medicine Hat to a place called Hilda where I had spent two lonesome winters. He stopped some yards from me, speechless with surprise, scratching his head. He held out his hand and started to pump mine. I thought I had grabbed a ham. Eddie was the foreman.

"For gosh sakes," he said, "what are you doing here?"

"I came out from Ontario to go ranching, Eddie. What are you doing?"

"I got married, left the farm and took this job."

"Well, I'm married too. My wife is in that trailer. We came to see Harry about finding a place."

"I heard there were visitors for Harry but never figured on you—for gosh sakes."

31

"Is Harry still a nice guy?"

"Just the best fellow in the world. Always the same."

"Think he can help us? Is he back yet?"

"He'll sure bust a gut trying. Came in late last night. You'd better look him up after breakfast. I've got to get chores done."

"Okay, see you later." And off Eddie went, still shaking his head in wonder and grinning while I hurried back to the trailer to wake Eleanor.

If Harry wondered just why a tired looking car and trailer with Ontario license plates had deposited an almost forgotten casual acquaintance on his doorstep, he gave no sign. Face to face with the first person who might put us on course, I became nervous and at a loss for words. It was important to sell ourselves and our sincerity to this man, our first contact in the west. Harry has a knowledge of ranches, ranching problems, developments and trends in the cattle business second to none. He had the power to send our illusions flying and our light-hearted expedition scurrying to the safety of another obscure city job.

These thoughts rushed through my mind as he smiled gravely and shook hands. I stammered that we had detoured this way to have a talk with him, but would be pushing on. If he could spare the time, would he listen to us? I guess he sensed that something was up, for he assured me he could find the time and insisted that having come to this remote spot we should not be in a hurry to rush on. I told him that what I had to say, and how he might react to it, had better take place before Eleanor. I told him it was terribly important to us, that Eleanor had just as vital an interest in the question as I had and begged him, before passing judgment, to hear us out first. Harry agreed to come around to the trailer for a meal that evening.

Eleanor remembers that we had hamburger for that fatal meal. I remember that she had the trailer looking cozy and homey as possible. We squeezed ourselves around the tiny table with Dane sleeping soundly at the other end. During the meal we sketched in our travels from the Swift Current days, enquired about mutual friends.

The meal over, we waited for Eleanor to clear away. We tried to settle ourselves comfortably. I looked at Eleanor and she looked at me. Harry remained calm and relaxed. We simply could not get down to business. And then out it came like a torrent—a wild jumble of pent-up cause and effect, the decision, the drive and the vague yearning to go ranching, to get on our own. Somehow Harry grasped the idea. Fortunately he had read 'The Compleat Rancher', knew R. H. Bennett and his ranch. But he did not enter into our innocent and perhaps imbecile discussion as we tried to convince him of our purpose. We were definitely trying to sell ourselves to ourselves against secret fears. Nor did he interrupt us as, in looking back on this desperate phase I am certain he might have, to point out that no one else to his knowledge had ever gone into the business in our condition and at our age. But, bless him, he said nothing that could so easily have spooked such a jittery couple as we were then. We finally dried up without putting forth, I am sure, one sensible point.

Then Harry began to talk, quietly and sincerely. He described the difference between ranches—the large spreads

33

in the short grass country with their big acreage and small carrying capacity, the small units in the foothills that could carry a family and support a cow on less land. He pointed to big ranches that changed hands frequently where one found sudden wealth or quickly went under. Then he explained the home life of the foothills ranch, the permanency and the stability. He warned us that we would never make a lot of money on the latter but always a good living. He spoke wistfully of the security and family team work on a ranch, the advantages of bringing up children, the deep satisfaction of working hard for oneself.

When we asked if he thought we could make it with insufficient funds and no experience, he pointed out that many others had started with less and the least we could do after coming this far was to try and find out if we had it in us. We tried to thank him and were assured he was delighted we had come to him for advice. He said we made him wish he were younger and that sometime tomorrow he would have a few suggestions to offer. After he left Eleanor and I talked late into the night, remembering too late the things we might have said. Isn't that always the way it goes?

Next morning Harry returned to the trailer. He felt sure that if we held to our present mood we would eventually want to settle in the foothills. But he was also very sure that neither of us knew whether we could stand the life-- being isolated, on our own, facing the problems and responsibility. How about a trial on one of the ranches? If he could place us with a good man, would we be willing to roll up our sleeves, work and learn, both of us? If we spent a winter cut off from all other interests in the short grass country and emerged in the spring with the same enthusiasm, he believed we would then be in a position to sell ourselves to the Veterans' Land Act officials for backing. And probably we would then know what type of country and what kind of ranch we wanted. It made sense. Turning to Eleanor, Harry asked if she would mind spending a few days alone in the trailer while he took me on a little trip. Eleanor welcomed a chance to stop in one place long enough to catch up with washing and mending. Harry had to inspect some experimental bands of sheep and if I joined the party we might, on return, look in on some ranches.

The party included Professor A. H. Ewen of Saskatoon and Dr. Rasmussen of Lethbridge. They inspected sheep at Manyberries, Scandia and Lethbridge. Acres, corrals and barns of sheep, technical talk of sheep, noise and smell of sheep—until I thought they would give me insomnia and began to wonder where this was leading. When the inspection finished at Lethbridge I got the point. Harry was going to run Professor Ewen into the Porcupine Hills out of Macleod to look at ranches.

It was a lovely day, clear and sparkling, when we headed for the Hunter Brothers' layout where they run purebred Herefords. Steve Hunter came along as guide. As we climbed into the hills Professor Ewen explained that he had spent the war in the army, had thought of the Veterans' Land Act and was interested in finding a ranch for investment purposes. He called this the promised land. I told him what Eleanor and I had in mind and picked up some advice I have never forgotten. "When you work around stock," the Professor said, "you will come across lots of jobs you won't like, and working with neighbours you will find many who can do the unpleasant chores better. Don't lean on them, make yourself learn and insist on doing these things yourself."

Toward the end of the day, after calling at some half dozen places, Steve Hunter declared: "I tell you fellows, **these ranches don't** change hands very often. There is one other I can think of where an elderly couple talk of selling. They can't exactly make up their minds, but it's a swell little place to look at if you want to drive that far. I think I can find a trail over these Porkies that will cut down the miles. It's on the west side." I was in the back seat not caring one way or the other but Harry and Professor Ewen decided to make this their last call.

There wasn't much daylight left when we got there, but you could see at a glance it was the prettiest setting of them all. The land sloped south, and off in the distance you could see the first range of the Rockies. Harry and Professor Ewen remarked on the bunch grass, black loam and the slopes that were laid bare of snow by the warm chinook winds. They were obviously interested and waited around to speak with the owner. Professor Ewen told me the price was fair and he would write the owner later about a deal. It was dark as we dropped down to the valley floor with the towns of Lundbreck, Cowley and Pincher Creek winking their lights in friendly fashion. I sat quietly in the back seat full of envy for Professor Ewen, his knowledge and experience, his position that enabled him to look at ranches for purchase. Some day it might be our turn, but we had such a long way to go. I thought of Eleanor and Dane patiently waiting.

If Eleanor could just see this country before settling down to an apprenticeship the sacrifice ahead would be easier to bear.

When we returned to Manyberries Harry got on the telephone. J. D. Gilchrist owned the Deer Creek Ranch of 32,000 acres, about fifty miles east. The married couple who worked there had just left. Joe was alone with one hired man. "I sent word you might be around for the job," said Harry. "Better leave in the morning."

Chapter Four

WE TOOK OFF early in the morning without the trailer, Eleanor map reading from a sketch of the route which Harry had made for us. There were few landmarks and no signs where the trails crossed as we worked east through badlands and deep coulees from one prairie flat to the next. At one junction Harry had marked on the sketch an old stove to indicate the turning point. When we found it we knew we were on course and wondered how many years it had been there and with what hope it had been transported into the country.

About noon we found the ranch house and saw Joe Gilchrist working in the corrals. He came up to prepare a meal and after we moved into the living room began to talk business. Joe explained that his family had a house in Milk River where the children were attending school. He had one man on the ranch who had been with him some years. He required a married couple as well, the wife to look after the house and meals, the husband to be chore boy and general ranch hand. As I began by explaining that Eleanor's cooking would more than make up for my lack of experience, Joe asked if I could milk a cow. I was afraid the truth might disqualify us and hastened to assure him I could. Eleanor glanced at me and I felt a tight little knot in my stomach. I hated myself for lying to Joe. He was a good guy and we took to him right from the start. When I confessed we were expecting another child and asked if it would make any difference, he said he had three of his own and was used to them. The wages he offered were $75 a month for the two of us. He showed us the bedroom we would use over the kitchen and said we could have the run of the house. We explained why we wanted the experience and agreed to take the job. I told Joe we had to drive to Medicine Hat so that a doctor could give Eleanor a checkover and that we would return in a couple of days with the trailer. He showed us where to park it. As we got into the car to drive away Eleanor was feeling awful. The strangeness of everything, the large house, the meals to prepare, the job she had to face in her condition—it was a tough prospect. Joe must have sensed that she was on the verge of tears. "Don't worry about us around here," he said. "We're not hard to get along with."

So this was to be our new home for a bit, a step in the right direction. I was feeling relieved that it was working out more quickly than we had expected. We had the right kind of job without having to detour into the hotel or restaurant business. But I was windy on one point. I couldn't milk a cow. Perhaps some time in the next few days I could pick it up at the Government station and Joe would never know. Although she was as ignorant as myself Eleanor said milking was easy. All you needed was a little practice. Anyway the obstacles were getting smaller and our courage was rising. We would meet our troubles when

39

they came, and not before. As we drove along we counted our blessings as Eleanor's mother kept reminding us to do.

However, just to prove it wasn't as easy as we thought and to hold out some tempting bait for a change of plans, fate hit us a couple of low blows. On the return to the station we had a flat tire about half way, some fifteen or twenty miles south of the settlement at Manyberries. Shortly after changing to the spare we had another flat! I began walking for help and had just disappeared from sight when I met a truck heading for Manyberries. We picked up Eleanor, Dane and the tires, were driven to the garage and returned to our car by a kindly man who refused any payment for his services. Well after dark, and very tired, we reached the trailer.

There was no rest in the morning. We had to reach Medicine Hat and the doctor. I checked the tires and they were all standing up. The spare was good. If they would just hold up for this last dash we would soon be at the Deer Creek ranch and our troubles would be over for some time. The car could rest. We waved gaily to Eddie and his good wife who had been so kind to Eleanor, swung around the yard and started to pick up speed when the engine fell to pieces! It was almost the last straw. After taking us West the old motor apparently felt it had done its job.

What were we going to do now? I wondered if we should call off the bargain at the Deer Creek. We were a good hundred and twenty miles from the Hat. I couldn't buy another engine, and if the car was beyond repair what chance did we have of getting the trailer out of here? Harry had told me that if we didn't take the job at Joe's ranch he would be delighted to hire me. A stockman was leaving.

The starting pay at the station was twice Joe's offer. Eleanor would not have to work and married quarters were provided. Nice little homes they were, too, with Eddie and Edna as neighbours. It was a chance to save money, to work regular hours. In time we could forget the risk of getting on our own or postpone it indefinitely as we settled into the steady routine. In her condition Eleanor would be safer here. Perhaps we should do the sensible thing and stop taking risks. All we had to do was move in and forget the car for the time. But a little voice said that if we really wanted to make things go our way all this was not so important as learning how to run a ranch from a man like Joe.

Eddie came along, looked at the motor, did some tests, decided it was a write-off and took charge. He had a truck going to Medicine Hat which could tow me in. It wouldn't cost a penny.

"But, Eddie," I said, "I can't get a new motor put in right away. We haven't got any of that green stuff left."

He just grinned and pointed out that car wasn't any good to us here. If we towed it to the city at least I could sell it. "I have to go in anyway," he said. "I'll take my car and bring Eleanor and the youngster."

He directed the truck driver to haul the car to a garage he recommended. I met him there and listened to the mechanic confirm Eddie's fears. They could rush a job on a new engine. Eddie took me aside. How much money could I pay down? I had about twenty dollars and the prospect of $75 a month at the Deer Creek. Eddie took me to the office, ordered a new motor, told them I would pay a little down and guarantee the rest in three months. He signed a note for me. Everyone was happy. In that town Eddie's word was gold.

He turned to me. "Now that's settled, is there anything else worrying you?" It had happened so quickly I hadn't had time to think. I tried to explain that we had some insurance and stocks but Eddie shook his head. "Leave your capital in storage. It's okay this way." And after making sure we had a place to stay he went about his business.

Eleanor, Dane and I walked to Tip Volway's store. We had a lot to tell him. But he had gone to the States where he had a horse racing. His two boys came up to give us a big welcome. Jack had been in the Air Force, and they told us their father had left instructions that if we called we were to be given the keys to the house. Philip drove us there, insisted on our taking the big bedroom, told us the kitchen was stocked with food and left us wondering what to do about it.

I picked up the telephone and called the clinic. Dr. Wilf Campbell, whom I had known since 1937 during my days in the police and who insists that all Campbells are related, was surprised to hear we were in town. He saw Eleanor that afternoon and after the examination agreed to take the case if she could get in to see him every three months.

The second day in town we visited a number of old friends. The car was ready the day after that and we drove back to the station.

While helping Eddie with some welding on the trailer hitch I remembered that I hadn't found the time for milking practice. Eddie pointed out the chore boy, an elderly Scot, and when he started for the barn with milking pails I sauntered up and asked him if I could help. He was suspicious, but when I told him I just felt like doing something he pointed to one of four cows. "What side of the beast do I sit on?" I asked innocently.

"Go on! You're joshing man," was his indignant answer. So I waited until he began milking and then tried to copy his technique.

I couldn't get any joy out of that cow at all. She didn't mind—at least she didn't kick—but I could get only a few drops at a time. Soon a crowd gathered, including some agriculture students from the university who demonstrated and explained before I retired, defeated. Eddie heard about it and convulsed himself laughing. Harry didn't let on that he knew. I felt it was a black mark against me and if Joe found out he would fire me in disgust. Eleanor thought it was very funny. After a final meal with Eddie and his wife we retired early for the drive to Joe's place next day.

Chapter Five

AT DEER CREEK the first thing I did was to have a heart to heart talk with the top hand on the ranch, Harold Haugen. I apologized for being the kind of dude that would ask too many questions and make his work harder by my ignorance. I told him that I knew nothing about the job but that I sure was willing to learn. He thought that was fine and said my attitude made it much easier for him. Then he told me of the hired men they had in the past who knew it all. They would send one out on a job and he would break something, or have a runaway, and they couldn't get things done the way they wanted. He said it was easier all around if he showed me the jobs the way he did them and I could follow the same pattern.

We got away to a good start. Harold broke me into the milking gently, but just the same I had to learn the hard way that you cannot bully a cow and have to come down patiently to her level of speed. Then he showed me how to harness the teams. When we started fencing I couldn't have had a better teacher, and Joe confided one day that Harold was the best man on fences he had ever had. Harold was a

44

perfectionist at everything and proud of his trade. We got along fine.

Then we divided the chores. It was always a job to beat Harold out in the morning. He would start the pump engine for the water system, fill the large stock trough, clean the horse barn and jump on the jingle pony to wrangle the horses from their pasture, cutting out from the string whatever we needed for the day. I looked after the bulls, chicken house, cow barn and, fortunately, just one milk cow. As soon as I got on to the job of milking one cow and had recovered from the equivalent of writer's cramp Harold brought in a second fresh cow, and it was like learning all over again. At the other end of this milk business Joe was teaching Eleanor how to look after the cream separator and clean the milk pails. Eleanor's early morning chores consisted of turning out a mass of hot cakes, eggs and bacon, which Joe considered the only breakfast fit to stay with a man during a morning's work on a ranch.

During those first weeks of apprenticeship something new had to be learned every day. Harnessing and driving teams, hoeing irrigation ditches, digging the large garden, hauling produce for the root cellar, shingling a roof, being blacksmith's helper at the forge, cleaning corrals and hauling manure, hauling and shovelling coal from the strip mine demanded long, hard hours of manual labour. We butchered a cow, and then a pig. I wasn't much help here and I didn't enjoy it at first. It reminded me of Professor Ewen's warning about unpleasant jobs and made me determined to learn.

After we had been almost two months on the ranch Harry dropped in unexpectedly, remained for a meal, and complimented Eleanor on her cooking. She was really doing

45

well. It was a treat to watch Joe lap up her Yorkshire pudding. By this time we were one big happy family, my back and arm muscles were not screaming so loudly, and it was easier to hit the floor in the morning and scramble around doing chores. But oh how we loved that extra hour in bed Sunday morning!

Harry wanted to know how we liked ranching. We were just beginning to realize how little we knew about it. When he asked me how I liked cow punching, I recalled that so far I had not even spotted the big herd nor had I been trusted on a horse for more than one casual ride with Joe. I wondered if I would ever get a chance to do some cow-boying. Then I shuddered as I remembered that one ride. Joe had taken me along to look for a stray bull. I dreaded the thought of separating from him for I might get lost and, moreover, if I did come across some cattle I was not sure that I could pick out a bull. Joe must have sensed my doubts for in his quiet way he said: "Surely you know what a bull looks like—he has horns."

Joe would generally disappear each morning on his Tennessee walking horse to ride his cattle and inspect the range. I figured it would be a long time before I graduated to that. Joe was tall, slim and youthful. On the lovely 'Friscoe', with his riding boots, special saddle and chaps, he was a sight to gladden the heart of any horseman. I would cast envious eyes in his direction when he set out and returned from his rides. Then one day he appeared with a second horse and called me over. "This is your pony," he announced. "I just bought him cheap. When you need a horse, ride this one. Get Harold to fix you up with a saddle and bridle and keep the same outfit."

As I led the horse away to the corral I called back: "What's his name, Joe?"

"Darned if I know—you give him one."

That night at supper Joe kidded me about my horse and asked what I called him. I decided to tag him 'Jughead' for no reason at all.

When we did get away from the barns and buildings Harold and I would proceed by saddle horse, truck or team and wagon. Generally it was a fencing job. I began to learn how to brace corner posts, tighten wire, splice wire, dig and tamp post holes, use an axe and drive a good staple. The ranch lay on both sides of the Milk River and we had to fence across the river at various points. Just when one job became tiresome we were able to switch to another, so there continued to be pleasant days of variety, instruction and hardening up for bigger things to come. There was always so much to tell Eleanor in the evenings. The years began to slip away. I hadn't felt so fit since I was twenty.

Joe had tried to retire once. The four Gilchrist brothers had worked together for years to build up a chain of ranches, and when they sold out Joe had tried living in town. When he found he couldn't get used to the pavement and hard sidewalks, missed the bawling cattle, the dust and action at branding time, the glorious sunrises and sunsets from the deck of a lively horse, he bought back the Deer Creek. He told us about one evening watching a thousand head of good Herefords grazing up the valley in close formation after a long drive, moving slowly west, the fading sun lighting up the bloom on their hides. We could understand his restlessness in town. A tall, bony, kindly man, at peace with

47

the world and himself, Joe was supreme on a horse, a picture of grace and rhythm working cattle.

Joe could inject fun into the deadliest jobs. Once while I was hoeing weeds in a bad irrigation ditch, and hating it, he came out for a few hours. I tried to keep ahead of him and whenever he worked down near me I would increase my efforts and move away. Finally he broke the silence with: "Hang on to one spot a little longer, so I can visit with you." But whether he was there or not you couldn't let up. You couldn't fool him; he was a smart cattleman and a shrewd manager. He knew exactly how long it would take to do a job and left one no time to wonder what to do next. In addition to being a prosperous owner Joe could do all the jobs on the ranch better than anyone else.

I like to remember the large fencing projects at the far end of the ranch or work on the telephone line. We would take the truck and a couple of saddle horses if there was river work. Into the truck would go the tools, posts, wire and grub box. Joe didn't believe in dull meals like tins of beans and spam with bread. The box always held a surprise. By the time we were hungry enough to eat a steer raw, Joe would get a good fire roaring, cook up a wonderful meal in a sheltered spot and we would have a royal picnic—tired, ravenously hungry and full of fresh air. These meals, eaten Indian fashion squatting or lying before the fire on a pair of chaps, the fall air crisp and clear, twisting smokes while we had those extra cups of coffee, were the highlights of the life on the Deer Creek. And Joe usually had some good stories to tell of the early days.

At the end of three months we drove to Medicine Hat for Eleanor's physical check-up. Everything was fine. Tip was pleased to see us looking so well. I also paid off the note at the garage for the motor. But we were glad to get back to the ranch.

When the first winter blizzards hit the country we climbed into our saddles with a vengeance. Crowding on extra sweaters, buckskins, coats, wearing chaps and 'neck rags', I began to feel that here, at last, was action. After an early breakfast the three of us would be off fording the icy river, rounding up little bunches of cattle together into a big drag and driving them miles into the teeth of the blizzard to winter grass. Joe taught me that you cannot get the feel of the weather by scraping the frost off the window and looking out at the bleak landscape or by reading the thermometer. If you hustled outside, properly dressed, and got right to work the cold was always much easier to bear than it seemed at first sight and shudder. When you were riding in open country, slowly stiffening up under the cutting wind and believed you couldn't go much farther, you had to hang on just a little longer to reach a coulee or river bank out of the wind. Often when you leapt to the ground from your horse the first impact was painful, for you couldn't feel your feet at all and imagined you were standing on stumps.

I found out how tough those range Herefords could be, what great little rustlers the weaned calves are. After the main bunch had been moved we went looking for stragglers. At one place we found a dozen big steers stranded on an island. They had forded the river to the island but the thin shore ice stopped them from returning. Having eaten all the grass and palatable bushes in sight to keep alive, they were now huddled together in a miserable phalanx, hump-ing their backs against the cold. We couldn't budge them until our horses had crossed and recrossed to mark a trail and break the ice. We had to do some riding and crowding to get them going, swinging lariats against reluctant hides.

It wasn't an easy winter for greenhorns but the tough spots were never so bad as we feared. We were a jolly crew, taking delight in wholesome fun. Joe was considerate and kind to Eleanor, more like a big brother than the boss. To Dane he was "Unca Joe". After lunch and a hard morning ride he would proceed to the living room for half an hour on the couch, waking up right on time. Then he would walk into the kitchen, look at Eleanor sheepishly and mutter apologetically: "Well, I had to rest my horse."

We had wonderful evenings in the living room with radio and books and good talk. We were more contented than we had ever been in our years of marriage. Joe let us send to Calgary for our trunks and cases of wedding presents that had been stored there since the Swift Current days. He trucked them forty miles to the ranch from the railroad and let us store them in an empty house. For the first time we had everything together.

When the Christmas holidays began Joe's wife Muriel and their three children arrived at the ranch. Dane was overjoyed at the games with his new playmates. Muriel and Eleanor together cooked up all sorts of surprises. The Gilchrists treated us as though we were their closest relatives. Muriel brought up the question of the baby's arrival in March and decided that a good three weeks in advance Eleanor should move to town with her, where trains and buses were handy for the dash to Medicine Hat. She insisted on having Dane too, saying she was lonely during the day with her three away at school. Dane and Muriel were firm friends from the start. He called her nothing but "Gilchwist".

Eleanor and I began to talk about the future. We wondered how long we could remain with these fine, understanding people without imposing upon them. Another child might make a big difference and it didn't seem fair to Eleanor or Joe. We felt it was time to get in touch with a Veterans' Land Act office and in January I wrote to Lethbridge. We reasoned that they could not very well advise us to return East or that we were unlikely to qualify since we were working for Joe and he was satisfied. We had to start some time.

The reply came that a field man would call the next time he was in the district. By the end of January I had sent them my discharge from the Air Force and my War Service Gratuity statement. We were very busy at the time hauling feed to the cattle and two extra men were in the bunkhouse with spare teams in the barn. We didn't have time to think about it, worry and plan. On February 14, 1947, we received an important communication. The regulations required the veteran desiring to be qualified to appear with his wife before the Regional Advisory Committee. Our appointment was fixed for February 25 at 2.45 p.m. in Lethbridge. This was our big chance if we were ever going to make the jump to a place of our own. With the way the weather was shaping up and the baby due in a few weeks it was running things pretty fine. I showed the letter to Joe and he suggested I combine the trip with Eleanor's move to town. In spite of

51

the heavy work we continued studying Professor Ewen's textbook on animal husbandry and in the evenings we had long talks with Joe in the attempt to prepare ourselves for any questions that might be asked to test our knowledge. We had to submit the names of three reputable stockmen who could vouch for our experience and ability and had picked as our victims Harry Hargrave, Joe Gilchrist and Eugene Burton of the V-T Ranch, known locally as the Will Rogers of Medicine Hat.

We had the car started early on the 25th to warm it up and managed to get to Milk River. We left Dane with Muriel and proceeded to Lethbridge. We were quite jittery about the test before us and poor Eleanor was terribly self-conscious of her appearance. I don't remember whether we had any lunch or what we did with our time until the 2.45 p.m. interview. I hoped with a fervour akin to prayer that we wouldn't let any of our friends down. If we couldn't impress these people it would be so hard to turn back, defeated. When we arrived at the office Eleanor puffed upstairs and I found her a seat on the bench where other applicants were waiting. I gave our name at the counter and glanced through the glass partition into the board room where the Government chairman was flanked by a prominent farmer and a rancher. At the other end of the long table a young couple were sitting on the edge of their chairs, the man twisting his cap nervously. I would rather have been waiting at a dentist's office for a long and difficult extraction. Would we be able to convince them?

Like all ordeals most of it was mental. The Committee were very kind and considerate. We stumbled over the questions about previous experience by remembering that Eleanor as a young girl had spent summers on a farm in England and I had done about the same in Ontario. As we talked about our present work I quoted Harry, Joe and Professor Ewen. When they went into my service in the R.C.M.P. I had an inspiration. For a time while stationed at Manyberries the Provincial Government had appointed me deputy stock inspector so that I could clear shipments of cattle out of the district. Obviously if the government had appointed me a stock inspector I must know something about cattle. I forgot to tell them I had been there only a few months. They were very pleasant and nice. At the end of the interview we shook hands all around and we were told that the Committee would write to us when they reached their decision.

Leaving Eleanor with Muriel and Dane at Milk River I returned to the ranch. We continued hauling feed, opening frozen water holes and fighting the cold. Joe took over as cook.

Then a curious thing happened. I must be careful setting it down because even for us, looking back, it is hard to believe. Fortunately I have the letters before me now. Remember that when we first arrived at Harry's station I had taken a trip into the Porcupine Hills with Harry and Professor Ewen. The latter had been very much taken with a ranch we found at the end of a long day of enquiry and inspection. Now a letter arrived from Professor Ewen dated February 27, two days after our ordeal before the committee, stating that with the acquisition of a house and daughter he was afraid he could not go through with a deal for the ranch we had seen. He thought the size would be right for us; the price was good and he sent me the post office address of the owner. Was this fate again, pointing the way? Joe thought we couldn't afford to miss any opportunity. I lost no time in getting off a letter to that address. Then I received a communication from the Veterans' Land Act dated March 1. The committee agreed it would be to our advantage to gain further actual experience by working on a ranch. It would be in order for us to work for Mr. J. D. Gilchrist for this season. Although the letter didn't turn us down it seemed to rule out the possibility of closing a fast deal. I continued working harder than ever on the ranch, feeling very fit and confident that everything would work out for the best. If I had time to think at all my concern was only for Eleanor. She had put up with so much to keep me happy that I could not fail her now, whatever the future had in store.

Muriel telephoned that Eleanor had left for Medicine Hat and everything was fine. Eleanor was shy about using the telephone and we agreed not to try getting in touch or writing until it was over. The days at the ranch merged into a blur of heavy slogging with frozen stacks and intense cold so that after the evening meals in the warmth of the kitchen I had to fight an inclination to drop asleep at the table. Outside all day it was a battle against the elements, a question of staying with it until the cold spell would break.

In the next mail that came through was a letter from the Porcupine Hills dated March 7. The owner of the ranch which Professor Ewen had recommended had decided to sell in the spring. He was getting on in years, had spent forty of them on his ranch, and I guessed the long hard winter had helped to convince him it was time to get out. He was asking ten dollars an acre and was running two hundred and twenty-five head of cattle through the winter. The ranch consisted of 1440 acres of deeded land, 160 acres of lease, with a permit to graze cattle on the forest reserve in summer. The school was two miles away.

I wanted to write or telephone Eleanor about it but remembering our agreement decided it would not be fair to raise her hopes. After all the Government had not qualified us and I was sure if we burst in on them so soon after the interview with a big deal pending they would get very sticky. But how about the present job? Would Joe want us to remain with two children? That brought me back to Eleanor again. It wasn't fair to think she could handle two jobs. Then I began to jot down figures on the back of an envelope. Assuming we could get the Government to approve the deal, what would their backing amount to? Their pamphlets stated they would pay up to $6,000 for a place if we put up ten per cent. We had twenty years to pay back the balance at a nominal rate of interest. That meant I would have to give them $600 first to get the six thousand. I put the car down at $800; we could cash in two insurance policies for $1,400; the trailer might sell for $1,000. And when I left the Air Force we had bought industrial stock now worth $1,400. That gave us $4,600. If the Government came in with $6,000 perhaps I could close the deal for $14,000. The difference between what I needed and what I might get was $4,000.

I didn't bother Joe about the details, merely showing him

the letter from the owner and telling him I could get within four thousand of buying it. He figured I should look at it anyway and told me not to worry about borrowing money to get started if it was a good place. He said that when he and his brothers started out they had borrowed a large sum on their name alone which had taken them years to pay off. I realized that even if we could swing it we would find ourselves with a ranch and no stock, but I hoped to be able to keep some of the owner's cattle on shares or make some kind of deal with a cattle buyer. I was ready for one more gamble. I remembered Eugene Burton saying to me in Medicine Hat: "If you find a good ranch and need help I'll throw in with you." Well, I had to drive to the Hat when the weather changed to get Eleanor. Perhaps Joe would let us run up and look at the place. It wouldn't be a crime to find out. It wouldn't cost us anything to ask.

As I came in with a sleigh at noon on March 20 one of the new men came out to tell me there had been a telephone call from Medicine Hat. Eleanor was fine and our family had increased. It was another boy—eight and a half pounds! Joe said he was our hot-cake baby. Howard Leslie, a neighbour, said: "That guy Campbell sure is getting set up for ranching. When he gets a place he's going to have lots of help." Eleanor wrote a letter five hours after the baby was born saying how thrilled she was, that he would be a fine rancher because he had such enormous hands. She had decided to call him Timothy Gray, she said, and he hadn't shown any objections. I began to write notes to everyone I could think of, in a few adding that we were going to look at a ranch.

Gradually the weather warmed up, but for quite a while the roads were too bad to attempt getting as far as Medicine Hat. Besides, Joe needed me. Finally, when the baby was three weeks old Joe thought I could get away that week-end and on the return I could drive around by Lethbridge. If things were breaking right he advised me to take Eleanor up to look at the ranch in the Porcupine Hills. Saturday morning we had to de-horn calves. As soon as the last one went through the chute Joe turned to me. "What are you hanging around here for? I thought you wanted to get away and see the new cowboy!"

I sprinted for the car without waiting to change clothes, reaching the house where Eleanor was staying two hours and forty-five minutes after clearing the first gate at the ranch. I had so much to tell my wonderful wife. It was spring, and we were going places. If we got the breaks.

Chapter Six

IT WAS COMFORTING to learn that Eleanor had been staying with Augie and Ethel Sauer. The day Eleanor entered hospital she had gone for a walk and dropped in to see Ethel. They had sat in the kitchen sipping tea and watching the alarm clock until it was time for Eleanor to go to hospital. Ethel had insisted then that she come to their home until I could fetch her.

Augie had arrived from Denmark as a boy to seek his fortune in the new world. He had done well as a cattle buyer and owner of ranches. He was a colourful character, a square shooter well liked by all stockmen in the South country. When I was in Manyberries as a young policeman trying to figure out what the job of stock inspector meant, Augie had dropped in to the detachment to have some carloads of cattle inspected. In the hungry thirties cattle on the hoof fetched only a few cents a pound. After buying a couple of carloads at the going rate, Augie then offered the rancher and his wife double the price for any steer or cow they could run through the living room! They managed to get one or two over the obstacle course. Everyone had a lot of fun and after that I am sure many more ranchers decided to sell their stock to Augie. He was friendly and considerate and I was always glad to see him in my district. We had fallen into the habit of having our meals together.

When we arrived in Medicine Hat from the East in the fall, I had spotted Augie driving down the main street and had followed him home. As Eleanor's mother was Danish, I wanted her to meet the big fellow. We had spent half an hour with them on that occasion.

And now here they were, the best of friends. Eleanor looked lovely that day. We stood at the door and gazed at each other with eyes full of pride and joy, Ethel beaming in the background and Augie booming: "Well, what are you doing out there? Don't you want to see your son?" He propelled us through the house to the bedroom where Timmy was asleep.

They left us alone for a big hug and Eleanor whispered: "My, but Ethel is a sweet person. They couldn't have been nicer to us and I have never been in a happier home. You would think the baby was theirs, the way they show it off to all the visitors. Oh, darling, is this world of ours full of wonderful people and how does it happen to be so perfect? Could we ask Augie to be godfather for Timmy? It's the only way we can thank them." I was pleased she had thought of that, told her this was the West and the people had always been that way.

We had a cozy visit. Sunday was beautiful, warm and sunny. As we relaxed in the goodness of their friendship all the tension went out of me. Augie complained about the treatment Timmy was getting. "The poor little fellow," he said. "That Timmy is sure being starved. Every time he cries he should be fed. I don't go for this old-fashioned feeding either. I like to see what they are getting—in a bottle."

We took pictures of the two families and then I told them about developments, being careful not to draw too glowing a picture of the ranch as I remembered it. Augie's opinion was definite. "You kids go to Lethbridge and talk to the officials. If you think it's what you want don't let anyone stand in your way. Then go up and see the old fellow at the ranch. Don't let them scare you or think you can't pay for it. Buy it if you can and worry about it after." If Augie had told me I could walk on the ceiling that day I would have tried it.

After getting away early Monday morning I found the chairman of the committee who had interviewed us two months before. This time we had more bounce. I explained that we had intended remaining with Mr. Gilchrist at least until the fall but the arival of Timmy rather complicated the arrangements. Then I told him about the ranch we wanted to inspect and how we had come across the lead. He said we had better tell our story to the Director, Mr. Miller, and get his opinion. We were shown into a private office. Mr. Miller appeared, all beams and smiles. Fortunately he had been to the ranch in question and knew the owner. He said it was a fine place. He checked our file again, said my name was familiar and wondered if we had not met when I was in the R.C.M.P. It would have been comforting to establish a friendly tie with the past but we could not connect any previous relationship. Mr. Miller said it had been worrying him since our case came before his office and some time he would get to the bottom of it. I fervently hoped that if there was something in my past it would not be bad. We didn't bring up the problem of financing the deal. Mr. Miller told us to go ahead and look at the ranch, then come back and see him. He didn't say yes and he didn't say no. So far we were holding our own.

We headed west towards the Rockies, but I couldn't have found the place unaided if we had been on a treasure hunt and my life depended upon it—which it did. At the Post Office we were told to cross the tracks and take the road north into the hills. The ranch was quite close, within twelve miles of the village the letter had said. The lady in the post office had mentioned Squaw Butte, and away in the distance we could see a height of land which might be the landmark. I watched the engine temperature climb as the car struggled up the hills and over the little bridges. Finally the road ended at a gate through which a track led into a hay meadow.

I opened the gate and followed the trail. The ranch looked larger than we had imagined. We were in a big green bowl with alpine slopes of clean, park-like grass on three sides topped with evergreens. There was Squaw Butte, sure enough, towering over us dead ahead with all the land sloping south from the rugged little peak. We spotted the house, a friendly, tidy building, freshly painted the colour of ripe corn trimmed with maroon and protected by a belt of trees. Off to one side was a new cabin. We noticed a large stock dam, a trim arrangement of corrals, barns and sheds. It looked awfully large and expensive, spread out there in a picture setting overlooking the valley behind us where strip farms reached to the Rockies about forty miles away. It was April 15, a heavenly day. Higher up patches of snow showed, clinging to the base of the trees and filling the coulees.

Eleanor held Timmy up, saying: "Look, darling. Daddy may get us a home after all." I didn't have to ask Eleanor how she liked the layout for her eyes were fairly shining.

But we were a frightened pair of youngsters. We knew without proceeding farther that this would exceed our wildest dreams for a place of our own. And having travelled so far, putting up with so much, the thought of losing it would be a major set-back. We debated whether to go ahead. It really looked like too big a proposition for our limited resources and all the backing we could get. We both felt we could look for the rest of our days and not find a setting that held so much appeal. Any other place would be an anti-climax. We should never be able to forget the perfection here before our eyes. I remembered the figures on the back of the envelope in my pocket. *If* we could sell this and *if* we could get so much for that. There were too many ifs! Turning to Eleanor I said: "Let's get out of here before we break our hearts."

As I turned around Eleanor stopped me: "No. Wait a minute. Remember what Augie said to us yesterday." We sat there in a panic of indecision until the owner came out of the house and waved us on. I put the car into gear and drove ahead.

While Eleanor went into the house with Timmy I travelled up the valley with the owner to feed some cows. It was just starting to green up; the earth was stirring sluggishly from its long sleep. Mr. Rhodes pointed to hay fields that were sod-bound and required working. The place had advantages of scenery, good grass and a temperate climate. The altitude couldn't be definitely established but we accepted it as around thirty-eight hundred feet. It was swept by the warm chinook wind, which bared the western slopes and high ridges for winter range. This was important. The disadvantages were lack of roads and schools. It struck me that the district abounded in small, family-size units where good homes were established. There were no large spreads of the kind that made fortunes overnight, yet the people had not been forced on relief in the hungry thirties.

When we began to discuss business I didn't dare look at Eleanor. We both felt we were there under false pretences. Mr. Rhodes told us that another party had sent word they were coming up to buy it but my letter had caused him to wait until he saw us. We made a lot of the fact he came from Yorkshire, some fifteen miles from Eleanor's home. He told us he would sell for $14,000 and agreed to go along with our deal through the V.L.A. if we could give him a definite decision soon. We got along fine that first interview and before leaving went over quickly some of the equipment now on the place, the things we would need for a start. Remembering the briefing Augie had given us I asked him to throw in a team and a set of harness. He hesitated but finally agreed. I promised we would let him know as quickly as possible after our interview with the V.L.A.

As it was too late to make Lethbridge we stayed that night in Macleod. Tuesday morning we were right on the button when the staff arrived. This time all the doors opened to Mr. Miller's office. By the way he looked at me I knew he had dredged up something from the days gone by. Thank heaven, there was a twinkle in his eye. He turned to Eleanor. "Mrs. Campbell, this may come as a surprise to you. I have

63

been digging through my scrap books at home. Here are some Calgary newspapers with pictures of your husband which may interest you. Let's see, it was in 1935 when Constable Campbell, your husband there, and three other Mounties shot it out with three bandits up in the mountains near Banff. Two of the policemen were killed as well as the three bandits. Now what you don't know, Mr. Campbell, is that the car the bandits held up in trying to get through the mountains to the coast, just before the shooting started, contained my brother-in-law and his wife, whom you do know."

From now on we had a friend in court. Mr. Miller could not do any more for us than for any other applicant but at least we could tell him everything. And we did. It appeared that we could split the ranch up, the V.L.A. buying and holding in our name half the ranch, or part of it up to the value of $6,000. We could make our own arrangements to buy the remainder for $8,000. It would all be our own when we had completed the payments to the government and ten years had elapsed. The clause withholding full title for ten years was apparently to stop a veteran from speculating on a quick sale.

We ran into more luck on this occasion. I told Mr. Miller that we would never be satisfied with any other ranch or type of country except the place we had found and that I was sure we could work out the details from our end. He advised us to get back up there as soon as possible and to have Mr. Rhodes sign an Offer to Sell listing the land and buildings. If the Offer was made for ninety days he would have it appraised and decided upon within that time. Then I brought up the question of our being qualified. By a

64

splendid coincidence the head man for Alberta, Mr. Allam, was then in the building. He agreed with the general idea of the deal. We stopped worrying about being qualified and, indeed, were only reminded of it when we received a certificate dated May 3.

As we drove back to the Deer Creek we speculated upon our chances of having the other knots untied as easily as this. We had to get Rhodes to sign the Offer to Sell but felt we should not mail it to him. While he was considering it someone else might appear with a better one. The trailer must be sold right away. We told Joe all about it and I got in touch with an agency in Lethbridge to sell the trailer. We soon got back in the groove working for Joe. He took a great interest in Timmy, insisted on getting breakfast for the crew several mornings a week and found time to help Eleanor with the dishes. We were now busy with irrigation. Harold was working at it from dawn until dark, and the days I helped him decided me that irrigation was fine anywhere but on our place.

I let one Sunday go by, then asked if I might take the trailer to Lethbridge. Joe didn't mind. I hoped to make a fast run, then continue on to see Mr. Rhodes and get him to sign the Offer. The day was very poor for such an ambitious trip, a steady downpour of rain and mud holes in the road. The old nemesis of flat tires dogged me this wet Sunday. I threw the first flat into the car and continued with the spare. The second flat forced me to walk some miles through the drizzle until I found a sheep man whom I persuaded to drive the tires to a garage farther on. By the time I had parked the trailer in Lethbridge it was time to start for home. I hustled south on the wet highway at dusk with headlights on. After some six or eight miles the car dropped into a large frost hole in the middle of the road, driving the radiator against the fan. The anti-freeze leaked over the road as I coaxed the car to the edge. I couldn't feel anything, or think. So I lit a cigarette. Just when everything starts clicking, this happens. I had a couple of dollars in my pocket. The best bet would be to start walking back to Lethbridge. Of all the miserable luck. I had been concentrating on an early return, giving Joe a good week's work before dashing off the next Sunday on the rest of the scheme. And here I was a few miles from Lethbridge with a broken radiator and fan.

A headlight showed coming from town and I got out to signal a stop. If the driver was going to Milk River perhaps I could hitch a ride and leave the car. To hell with it.

A new ton truck pulled up and a pleasant looking man stepped out. I explained my trouble, making the point that I had to be back to work for the next day. The chap looked at the damaged radiator, shoved his hat on the back of his head and agreed I was in a jam. I asked him how far it was back to Lethbridge, thanked him for stopping and told him I could probably get a garage in town to look after it.

"I've got a better idea," he said. "We can tow it to my place a few miles farther on. In the morning we can take the radiator off and find out the extent of the damage. If it needs special work we can run to town and get you on the way by noon tomorrow."

When we reached the farm and entered the cheery, modern house I realized this man was a big grain farmer.

"My name," he told me, "is Russell Greeno and I'm sure glad you are here to keep me company. Just drove the wife to the hospital. Expecting a baby tonight and I hate to be alone with the kids."

He let me use the telephone and I spoke to Eleanor, explaining the latest misfortune with the car. Then Russell and I had supper. We slept together and talked late about our interests, our wives and children. He knew Augie Sauer, was interested in our story, told me about his own start and what he had achieved. It worried him that he couldn't buy the trailer or help us in some way. He was genuine and sincere.

As we were having breakfast the telephone rang with the good news that the Greenos had a baby girl. Russell was an excellent mechanic and soon had the radiator off and the fan fixed. We took the radiator to Lethbridge where Russell kidded an expert repairman into doing a quick job and not charging too much. While I waited he nipped around to the hospital. Back at the farm he installed the radiator and had me going so soon that I was able to get back to the ranch for afternoon chores. In telling Eleanor about the kindness of Russell, who had asked me to keep in touch, let him know how things turned out, and by all means to drop in with the family the next time we should be that way, the grief of the previous day was forgotten.

When I explained to Joe my bad luck in not getting Rhodes to sign the form he advised me to keep after it. So I took a chance and mailed it, trying to forget the details hanging over us, the figures and the sharp pencil work Eleanor and I had gone over time and again. Revising and

hoping, one minute burning with conviction that everything would work out, the next minute in the depths of
misery over the gap of at least four thousand dollars that
made it seem hopeless, we waited fearfully for Rhodes' reply.

The calves were arriving, and with irrigation in full
swing we tried to submerge our doubts in hard work and
give Joe better value for our presence. The next week-end
Muriel and the children came out to the ranch, so we had
no time for conferences or plans. The mail arrived on
Saturday. A thick letter was addressed to Eleanor and
myself. As she was busy in the kitchen I sneaked over to the
bunkhouse to read it after the noon meal.

I had to go over that letter three times before it would
sink in. And then I couldn't believe it. A cheque had
fallen out of the envelope, but when I retrieved it with
shaking hands my eyes couldn't make out the figures. I
wiped the moisture away, fumbled for a cigarette, got hold
of myself and read the letter for the fourth time. I must be
dreaming. If this was true, could I make Eleanor believe it?
The writers said they had followed our journeyings with
great interest and congratulated us both on the arrival of
Timmy. They thought the work we were doing and the
sacrifice we were making was worth while and the news that
we had found a ranch had made them wish to speculate on
our venture. It was heartening to think that a young couple
today would cut the strings of modern living in the city to
go back to the fundamentals that had built up this young
country. They had come to the conclusion, although we
had not asked for help, that it would be fun if they could
come in on the adventure. Would we tolerate silent partners
if the government had no objections? They enclosed a

68

cheque for $5,000, but if this was not quite enough we were to write and say so. The letter pointed out that if we had decided to start out in business, running a bowling alley or a string of tourist cabins, they would not have been interested in the least. But the thing we were striving for seemed to them to be as good for Canada as developing a new oil field. They would be much happier to have this money at work helping our plans than in a bank to be invested in something they would never hear about.

Nothing like this had ever happened to me before. How could one say thank-you for a letter like that? Eleanor would find it impossible to believe if I told her verbally. This girl from England who had left security and social position to keep a restless husband happy in search of an indefinable longing for a way of life, after all the wandering and uncertainty, the work and struggle, would she see this as the turning point? I walked slowly over to the house. I couldn't take Eleanor away for a talk. It would have been fun to interrupt the house full of guests and share this letter with Joe and Muriel. But somehow the letter seemed sacred, its message for us alone. Eleanor had to go through the experience of reading it alone first. I tried to calm myself, slipped the letter to her and whispered that she must go off by herself to read it. I am afraid it alarmed her, for it might just as well have been bad news and I gave her no hint of the contents. But I am sure she shared it with Timmy when she was feeding him. The rest of the day he was perfectly contented and good as if all the tension in his Mummy had given way to calm and peace.

These good people insist on being anonymous. They consider their help only a small part of the story. And they repeatedly assure us they have been more than repaid in the letters that flow continually from us. But they have been firm on one point, that we should write down the tale of our adventure to encourage others. And because they have saved all our letters I am able to quote part of Eleanor's reply after receiving this thrilling information that removed so much of the risk to our plans. As you read her conservative lines please bear in mind that she had been overwhelmed time and again by the kind words and actions of the Burkes, Whytes, Volways, Hargraves, Gilchrists, Sauers and a legion of good Samaritans.

Eleanor wrote: "I know I can't put on paper all that I feel and would like to say. In all the rush of this week-end with never a chance to discuss things with Gray, he and I have shared, undeclared, the purest happiness and peace knowing that these dreams and plans of ours are coming true, with nothing to stop us now, only made possible by your wonderful offer. Why you should want to do this for us I will never understand. With you two for partners we shall have all the greater incentive to make a success of the venture. I know I feel I could lick the world now! . . ."

It was time we stopped running around in circles. If we were ever going to make the jump, this was the moment. We were not the same pair that had arrived at Harry Hargrave's the previous September. We laughed at the memory of our predicament when the motor packed up and we thought about working on the station. Joe had shown and taught and shaped us to appreciate the real values of life on a ranch, the balance between the financial and spiritual dividends. Everyone with whom we had come in contact had added something of value to our new character.

If we worked hard and continued to learn we might be as happy and contented as Joe, not striving for supremacy over the next man, neither jealous of a neighbour nor dissatisfied with our lot. We could be so wrapped up in our own little world of creation that we would actually be at peace with the rest. These thoughts made us very humble.

We wanted to go on but hated to leave the Deer Creek. We discussed the possibility, in making the deal for the ranch, of asking the owner to remain there during the summer while we stayed on with Joe until after haying. We put it up to him.

"It will take you all summer to get the feel of the place before winter closes in," he said. "I could use you here but you'd better get settled as soon as you can."

We had to make one more trip into the hills. If we could persuade the owner to let us move in and begin working the place while the V.L.A. wheels started grinding, we could pick up all our cases, trunks, boxes and bags and move for the last time.

Chapter Seven

THIS SUDDEN CHANGE of fortune bewildered us. All the details, the difficulties, the juggling around with figures trying to make the impossible happen disappeared into thin air. From the mere fact of our now having money or convertible assets to make the purchase possible we assumed that everything would soon be settled. Looking back, this sounds like utter folly but we had never been so certain as now that the scheme must fall into a pattern of our choosing. It had to go our way. We began jumping ahead of ourselves in our plans.

Not until we were speeding along the highway the following Sunday towards *our* ranch did we realize Mr. Rhodes had not returned the Offer to Sell which had been mailed to him. We were pulled back into the same old rut, however, when we had two more flat tires. A Sunday driver took me to Macleod to have them patched and a taxi returned me to Eleanor and the stranded car. Early in the afternoon we turned off the highway for the climb to Squaw Butte.

As we imagined or as Joe had warned several parties had

been after the ranch since our first visit. As the roads improved we could expect more visitors to build up the opposition unless we acted quickly. Mr. Rhodes told us one of the parties had offered more money! Hoping it was an offer of part cash with time for payment of the balance, we said that we were ready now for a straight cash deal. We added that the Director of the V.L.A., whom Mr. Rhodes knew, would be coming up soon to complete the business as we had agreed. We acted as though it was taken for granted our offer stood and for the moment we did not mention the Offer to Sell.

We spent the night in our home-to-be. Eleanor and I slept little, whispering to each other the things we wanted to see and ask about, the strategy and line of talk we should adopt in getting the paper signed. We kept running to the window to look at the view in moonlight so bright we could see the Rockies. Then we would do a ghostly jig, throwing our arms wide and trying to shriek at each other in an excited whisper: "Just think! It is almost ours."

Next morning when we asked Mr. Rhodes to drive around with us he suggested we view the summer range and the farm land. The summer field looked immense.

"Does all this belong to the ranch?" I asked.

"Oh yes. There is just as much again over the hill," he said. We had not grasped the acreage involved and were quite awed to think of all the land we might own one day. To Eleanor it all seemed more lovely on this second trip, perhaps because she had not dared to let herself go the first time she viewed it. Now that the place was within reach she began to take it all in. She had a good look at the house as well and decided it had possibilities.

The visit had gone very well, but before we left it was necessary to find out exactly where we stood. Should we be business-like and precise, asking for a straight answer, or would this afford them a moment for pause and doubt? Or should we try a little gentle psychology? The Rhodes were an elderly couple. Several people had warned us that they had been on the point of selling two or three times previously and had backed down at the last minute. Obviously they were attached to this place and would be reluctant to leave the home to which they had devoted the best years of their lives. Perhaps the other prospective purchasers had been too anxious about how soon they could move in and take complete possession. If the owners could be made to feel they were wanted and welcome around the place for an indefinite time they might not panic at the thought of finally having to leave their ranch for good. If this reasoning was correct they might not back out of the deal once again. It looked to me as if this was the best method of approach. We had returned to the house and were seated in the kitchen.

"Mr. Rhodes," I said, "we will never find another ranch as nice as this. We can appreciate how you picked the site, homesteaded, added and improved upon it so that it will always be known as the Rhodes' place. Eleanor and I can understand how you and Mrs. Rhodes must feel at having to part with it. You know how we have worked to find a place like this. We would like to buy it and carry on the work as you had planned. If you would like us to be the

74

new owners Eleanor and I would be grateful if you could both stay on, at least until the hay is up, to advise us and show us how you operated. We would not like you to feel you had to move away and lose contact. You will want to spend your winters in comfort and security without the work and responsibility, but you will always be free to return and visit when you wish. If you would like to sell under those conditions we will move up here in a week or so with our things and live with you. It will take the V.L.A. a little time to complete the deal. In the meantime we can be working the place together. When the place changes hands it would be a great help to us if you remain here so we can have the benefit of your advice. How does that plan strike you?"

"That's the way I want to sell," he said. "We don't want to begin thinking of a place to live right away. After forty years in one spot it is hard to move in a hurry at our age. If you would like me to stay I will be glad to see you settled in and help in the running of the place."

"Well, that's fine," I said. "Until the deal goes through we will be helping you. In the meantime you have got yourself a man and you don't have to pay wages. We will share the food costs. Mr. Miller, Director the V.L.A. in Lethbridge, will have the ranch appraised in a month or two and then they will buy it for us. He asked me to have you sign the Offer to Sell form which will start the ball rolling."

The form was filled in, signed and witnessed. I told Mr. Rhodes that through the V.L.A. he would be paid in full for the ranch. That would leave us with the place but without any stock. We talked about keeping some of his cattle on shares but he was not too keen. He did say, however, that he would sell us some cows with calves, thirty or forty head, and he would give us four years to make three annual payments. It looked to us as though we had everything covered.

At this stage although the excitement we felt was terrific we had to keep it suppressed. The tension had made us jumpy. Living that moment over again, it is amusing to find a calm and factual letter Eleanor wrote to our silent partners describing the visit with the following postscript: "Both boys approve of the ranch. Timothy slept like a top the whole time we were up there and after Dane had looked the place over he said: 'Well, let's go back and get my toys!' "

Driving to Lethbridge with the precious paper Eleanor and I tried to recall the things we had seen, the surprises in buildings, the fine cattle, the lovely scenery that unfolded from any angle, the dream-like quality of our amazing luck. Then we took hold of ourselves. We were committing the rest of our youthful years to hard work, no luxuries, precious little furniture. Our own interests would have to be subordinated in paying off every cent. Yet we were going into it with joyful hearts. Joe had taught us what was ahead, working from dawn to well after dark—no forty-hour week, no holidays—seven days a week. If we weren't dragged down the first few years by crop failures, drouth or falling prices we knew we could weather the storm. There would be no time out for illnesses—we couldn't afford to be sick. The Government was giving us twenty years to pay back their loan and we hoped to have the silent partners repaid in three to five years. But when it was all cleared, look at what we should have! A fine little family ranch, real stability for our children, a business in which they would grow and develop, all cleared for them if they should decide to carry on. And best of all, a place for us to retire with the help of the boys. Oh yes, even then we had decided this was where we wanted to spend the rest of our days. We should then have a little cottage where in the declining years we would have the comfort and luxuries we were prepared to do without now.

Back in Lethbridge we waved the paper before Mr. Miller. He congratulated us and said it was indeed a fine spread. I warned him about Rhodes backing out of deals in the past and said we were moving in within a week if we could to work with him. Because of the bad roads during the winter the office was behind with the appraising and it would normally take five or six weeks before they could get around to our choice. Mr. Miller was prepared in view of this to try to come up himself within two weeks.

Eleanor dragged me straight to a store to buy garden seeds, saying: "Mr. Rhodes had the garden all ploughed and ready. I can hardly wait to get my hands into that lovely black loam."

We were treading on air. "How about it, El?" I said. "Are you ready to move for the last time? Would you like to change places with anyone in the world at the moment?"

"I really can't believe it, but I hope to come down to earth in time to get the packing done."

Somehow she managed it, and if Joe ever reads this I trust he will realize with what sadness our joy was tinged at leaving the Deer Creek and the fine people there. Muriel and the children were coming out next week-end and we tried to get a truck to help us move the following Tuesday or Wednesday. However, the storekeeper in Milk River who was arranging for this transport telephoned Saturday afternoon with the information all trucks were busy during the week and he had managed to get one to take us Sunday!

We had a real send-off. A three-ton truck was piled high with our cases and trunks. Joe gave us a sack full of seed potatoes for our garden and as we all gathered before the house to move off, called out: "Just look at them! They drove in here with a few suitcases last fall and now they are pulling out with half the ranch."

Eleanor couldn't let it go with a handshake. She turned to the wonderful "Gilchwist" and said: "Muriel, do you mind if I kiss Joe good-bye?" And to Joe: "Is there any rule against kissing your cook?" We were all feeling sad. If we hadn't turned to go at that moment tears would have been in evidence. This was the first time we did not enjoy moving on.

The first week we were busy getting settled, storing our things on the verandah and in two small bedrooms in the main house, helping with the chores and gardening. On Wednesday Mr. Rhodes went to town to see his lawyer. On his return he told us about meeting a rancher who had just heard he was selling. When the fellow realized we were here waiting for the deal to be completed he told Rhodes he was coming up to offer us cash to change our minds. Mr. Rhodes then told us that six other parties were after the ranch, including some from the States. The weather turned wet, the roads became impassable and we spent too much time sitting around wondering if the appraiser would get out.

On the following Sunday I helped two neighbours brand their calves. The next afternoon I started riding for the mountains with the spring cattle drive. We stopped the night at another ranch, started at daylight with the neighbour's bunch added to ours and picked up a third neighbour with his cattle on the way. It took all day to trail them about twenty-five miles into the mountain forest reserve. We spent the night in a cabin with the Stock Association rider, talking of horses and cow men, sleeping in saddle blankets on the floor. It was a trip to remember always and afforded escape from the tension of waiting developments.

We rode straight home the third day and to my dismay I learned the appraiser had been out. It was unfortunate that I had not been present to answer his questions and he did not seek the answers from Eleanor. She was worried, and more than that, apprehensive. Mr. Miller, to whom we had told so much, did not make the trip and it was obvious the new man did not have all the details. He told Rhodes this was the largest deal the Government had handled so far in the district. To complicate matters a quarter section of land adjoining had been sold for $18.50 an acre. Our ten dollars an acre deal was pending, but what if there should be a loop-hole somewhere?

I questioned Eleanor further. She said the man had been here most of Tuesday and as he was leaving she ran out to ask him what she should tell me. He said some papers would be mailed for me to sign. I was very tired from the long ride, confused with the various accounts of the visit from the appraiser. It didn't sound right. Could there be further obstacles to jeopardize our slim chance for success? I did not believe so, but Eleanor felt our plans were approaching a crisis.

The first thing that resulted from the inspection was a letter asking for more details on my financial standing and working plans. Curiously enough at the same time Rhodes told me he could not sell us any cattle on time as he would have no guarantee of payments. The coincidence was significant but we were not disturbed. Once the deal was through I was positive that Augie Sauer or some Medicine Hat rancher like Eugene Burton would offer just as good a proposition. I sent an account of our financial standing to the V.L.A., mentioning the silent partners, telling them everything we had explained to Mr. Miller. I sold the car quickly for $900 and purchased a second-hand army jeep. The agency got rid of the trailer for $1,200. We sent off letters about cashing our insurance policies. We sold all our personal effects we could market in a hurry, including a new suit of mine and Eleanor's electrical appliances. I hated to part with a fine leather suitcase that had travelled with me since September of 1939.

The appraiser had obviously found a lot of loose ends. We had believed his job was concerned only with the state of the ranch and its earning capacity. Why should the V.L.A. be writing at this stage for more details? We had told them everything, they had allowed us to move up here and nothing had changed our standing since then. Well, we had sold the car and trailer; everything we owned was here. But time was running out on the Offer to Sell. Mr. Miller had certainly been wise in advising us to make it for ninety days. They would have to use dynamite to get rid of us, we were so well dug in. But the delay was giving the owner understandable concern. After we had moved to the little cabin other buyers began to appear openly and sessions went on in the main house. We began to look like squatters and cold fear began to displace our high hopes. We now had just enough money to buy the ranch and if any other conditions were imposed we should be at a loss to meet them. We began to suspect everyone. Mr. Rhodes tried to call off the deal and offered to pay us for our time working as ranch hands. He was very positive that we could make no deal for cattle with him or anyone else except on a cash basis.

It was almost the end of June when the roof fell in. A letter from the V.L.A. stated that after reviewing our case the Board could not proceed further unless we could stock the ranch with forty head of cows and their calves owned by ourselves. They had to be convinced we had a reasonable chance for a financial return the first year. We stopped fencing, farming and gardening long enough to realize we were in a spot such as we had never before experienced. I felt a very real persecution complex for the first time and said to Eleanor: "You know we are licked. Let's retire in dignity while there is still a chance to get out of this mess without hurting anyone else."

"What kind of people do they think we are?" she said. "No one is going to push us around now. You had better start for town and keep going until you come back with an answer. I'll hold the fort here. If both of us leave now our stuff could be put off the place, but I think we have some kind of common law rights as long as we hang on. Besides I have put the garden in."

Next day I left for town and I wasn't coming back without an answer. That's what the girl said. My girl.

Chapter Eight

LET US PAUSE for a minute to consider our state of mind. We felt the world had turned against us, not the world of our friends but a world of officialdom and strangers. Our friends were far away and at the moment they were the last ones I wanted to see. It was a funny sort of persecution complex. There wasn't anything definite you could put your finger on, but a number of little incidents, piled on top of a good imagination, began to add up. Strangers in a new country, we were being called with a weak hand. We were so close to getting the ranch and winning our objective that this new condition of buying a bunch of cows and calves first seemed an obstacle of major proportions. Once the ranch was in our hands I could go anywhere and buy cattle or take them on shares. It was an easy sort of deal to swing. But to make the purchase of the ranch conditional on my having cattle first, before I had the ranch to bargain with, knowing the exact state of our finances, was to my mind at the moment tantamount to telling us we could go no farther. The cards were definitely stacked against us. If I had been in a reasonable frame of mind and had driven to Lethbridge first we might have threshed it out. Understandably or not I was very sure someone in the Government was waiting to pounce upon me and talk me out of it. I am telling you this so that we can be fair in relating the next incident. What was I to do?

I don't believe Eleanor fully understood the seriousness of our financial position. When she told me to drive away and come back with an answer that would satisfy the authorities, she had probably been made overconfident by our amazing luck in the past and felt I could pull another miracle. I had been caught up in her mood and felt I would return with the solution. But driving along the highway, not thinking very clearly, the old doubts and fears took hold. In the back of my mind was the certainty that once the ranch was ours we could work out any kind of deal. As the matter stood we were on the brink of disaster.

I turned into Pincher Creek. Was there any use in going to the Canadian Legion and talking to fellow veterans? I didn't know any of them well and besides they had their own troubles. The lawyers in town were working for Rhodes. I did not know any business men and there were no ranchers around to whom I could turn for ideas. With a chip on my shoulder from nervous apprehension and no clear plan to argue from I went into the bank, asked to see the manager.

"It's like this," I said. "We are on a good little ranch and the V.L.A. approves, but they won't complete the deal unless I own forty cows and calves. I have enough money to buy my share of the ranch but nothing for livestock."

The manager shook his head sadly. "You veterans read these pamphlets overseas and look at the nice pictures and imagine how wonderful it is going to be when you get home. But it isn't like that at all."

"Is there any way I can buy some cattle?"

"Yes," he said. "The best proposition for you is a farm improvement loan. You pay ten per cent down on the cattle, the Government guarantees the rest and you pay off the loan in a certain amount of time at a reasonable rate of interest."

They had me there too. I would have to borrow more money but had never in my life been in so deep as I was at the moment. The V.L.A. would probably take another look at the picture and turn thumbs down. The bank manager had correctly pointed out there was no guarantee that cattle would not go down in price. Everyone was sure there would be a post-war recession and no one was expecting it more than the rancher. To base the purchase of this ranch and its survival on the buying of forty head of stock, with prices expected to go down, and tie it up with anything as strict as a bank loan was simply courting disaster. I didn't want any of it. So I left.

It took me a few years to learn that the bank manager was himself a veteran of World War I, that he was a hell of a good guy and that it was time somebody pulled me up short with a few home truths. I didn't enjoy it at the time but I have realized these facts since. Everyone else had been patting us on the back, increasing our daring and elan. This man made me realize that the ranch with its potential earning value was sitting on one side of the scales and borrowed capital on the other, nearly in balance. One bad decision or a freak change in our fortune would upset it. I recalled Professor Ewen's last letter in which he warned me that we had to buy a ranch now. We could not afford to wait for the prices to go down. And he had it figured that there were three years of steady prices ahead in which to reduce our capitalization. Against this I remembered the words of Gene Burton: "Don't let the banks get into you, fella. Lots of us old timers spent our best years working our heads off for the bank." And there was Eleanor holding the fort with the simple faith that I would wheel up to the door, jump out waving my arms and call: "Everything is fixed, Buckwheat! We are saved again!"

Walking down the street of this prosperous little town I wondered where to turn. For the first time I was alone and frightened, a complete stranger. The nearest friends who knew what we had been through were almost two hundred miles away. As I crossed the street a big smile lightened the face of a passing priest and a strong hand grasped mine. What on earth was I doing here and why did I look so worried? He was a husky Irishman who as a student had played such good baseball in the States a semi-pro team had tried to sign him up. But he had become a missionary priest and taken a vow of poverty. We had been good friends when I was in the R.C.M.P. and he was working in the relief-stricken coal mining areas of the south. Although I was a Scotch Presbyterian we had shared an interest in sports, books and common experiences in our work. He had seen me off to war and we had exchanged a few letters. But that was years ago.

I told him the story briefly. Now he looked worried. We climbed into his car and drove away from the town to park and talk it over. He said if he had some time to work on it he might rally some help. I told him we couldn't borrow money as we were already involved too deeply. He reminded me of his vow of poverty, but said he owned this car and offered to sell it so I could put up a payment on cattle. His attitude gave me courage. I told him we might lick it some other way and we parted with his promise to come up and help with the haying. I think that I revealed some of my persecution ideas or the suspicion of a double-cross into his mind, for he reacted as a good fighting Irishman would. When I left him I was ready for another round and just waiting for the bell.

Driving back to Cowley I decided to telephone Eleanor. But what could I tell her? We couldn't waste time, every day was valuable, and here I was cruising around. I had settled nothing. If a solution could be found I would have to drive to Medicine Hat to find it. I thought of Augie and his voice booming: "You kids buy it if you can and worry about it after." I thought of Tip and his infectious enthusiasm. They would be the boys to see.

At the telephone office in Cowley I put through a call to Augie's house. Ethel answered, said Augie would be in that evening. This was Saturday. I told her I was leaving Cowley right away and would drive straight there. She said Augie would be waiting for me. Now I had something to tell Eleanor. I put through a call to the ranch for my wife. The operator turned to me and said: "I have spoken to the ranch but Mrs. Campbell isn't there any more."

I blew up at that piece of information. "Sure she's there," I said. "She was there when I left this morning and is expecting me to call." The operator rang again, told the party at the other end to have Mrs. Campbell come to the telephone right away, or else! It was good to hear her voice.

87

I tried to sound cheerful. Was she all right? Fine. I was just leaving for Medicine Hat. I had something cooking. Augie was waiting to see me. I would return as soon as I possibly could. Eleanor was equally cheerful. She would hang on, and here's to success. We couldn't say any more.

I burned up the road to the Hat, giving the old army jeep everything it had and arrived about eleven. Augie was waiting and we talked until about three in the morning. Augie got mad. "What's the matter with that bunch in Lethbridge? Why can't they let you buy the place and leave you alone to run it your own way? We'll get the cattle for you, don't worry about that." I tried to explain about the series of incidents that made us think we were being squeezed out of the deal and although we couldn't pin down any evidence of connivance between all the parties concerned, unless I could come up with something solid for the V.L.A. Board, with no loopholes, they might withdraw once and for all. Augie was distinctly embarrassed. "Right at the moment I can't help the way I would like to," he said. "All my money is tied up until next winter in cattle."

"Believe me, Augie, the last thing I wanted from you is financial help. I drove down here because there isn't a friend in that country I could talk to, and you know the angles. Maybe you could come up with an idea I haven't figured."

I had not eaten since breakfast and Augie cooked up a meal. "Let's go to bed," he said finally. "Maybe we can sleep on it and come up with a plan in the morning." It was very late and I had a splitting headache, but in that friendly home I slept like a baby.

I was awakened by the aroma of bacon and eggs and good coffee. Ethel was cheery and full of fun. We had a pleasant breakfast. She would not let us talk business or worry until the meal was finished. As Augie and I twisted smokes in the living room I knew by his silence that he was worried. I began to feel badly about coming down to bother him like this with our troubles. Finally he looked up.

"What do you figure we should do first, Gray?"

"I don't know, Augie, but I remember Tip Volway told us when we had our ranch one of the big fellows in the short grass country would give us a start with cattle. I don't want to do it this way but if I could show on paper that I had these cattle, and no strings attached, I think we could force the thing through. It won't be long until the time limit is up on the Offer to Sell."

"Let's talk to Tip," he said. "Phone his house and ask him to meet us down town."

I called the Volway house, told Tip I had a knife in my back and someone was getting ready to twist it, that Augie and I had been trying to get it out and we would like to see him if he could get down town. He said he would drive right to his store and we could talk in the office.

We started to toss it around once more. It seemed like an improper subject on this peaceful Sunday morning. I was sick and tired of the whole thing, but they were a couple of great guys who had gambled with life and won. They were getting their teeth into it. When I mentioned one of the big ranchers trusting us with the cattle Tip thought it was a good idea.

"To hell with it," said Augie. "We can do it right now without leaving the office. I haven't got much loose money, but say we each put up five hundred dollars and telephone a few other guys for the same amount. How about that, Tip?"

"Sure," said Tip, "we can get it covered in half an hour." And he grabbed the telephone.

"Wait a minute, fellows," I said. "Eleanor and I would rather give up the ranch than borrow money from you boys. I didn't drive down here for that. Joe Gilchrist and others told me about starting up like this and getting a bank behind them on their name alone. This country is healthier than it was in those days and there wouldn't be as much risk for a bank. I bet a good manager who is interested could help me convince the V.L.A. and put the thing across. And I'm willing to bet with his prestige and the right amount of bluff we won't have to sign papers or borrow until we have the ranch in our hands. Eleanor and I don't care how hard we have to work as long as we can leave the ranch cleared of debt for our boys. The whole problem is to find someone like that with enough nerve to help me cut the red tape."

Tip jumped to his feet. "I've got it!" he said. "You know Hutch, Augie. He was a bank manager here for some time. Right now he's in Lethbridge waiting for a new branch to open. He always wanted to be a rancher and he knows the business. Besides, he will probably have more authority to take chances looking for new business."

Tip chuckled as he picked up the telephone. "This is the kind of thing he likes and if he can't work it out nobody can." He put through the call. "Hutch? This is Tip. What are you doing, sitting around in the hotel? Look, I've got a friend here in the office. You don't know him but he's got

90

a problem. Sure, I'm sending along a new customer for the bank. Can you see him today? Okay. Listen to his story and give the boy a break. If you want any backing I'll sign any notes you agree on."

Augie grabbed the telephone. "This is Augie Sauer speaking. I want to sign the notes too." When Tip had hung up we parted at the front of the store. I raced around the block, found I needed gasoline and pulled into a service station. While I was checking the tires a car stopped at the corner. Tip's head appeared through the window opening and he beckoned me over. "Did you have something to eat, boy? I forgot to ask. Do you need any cash?" I told him I had enough but he shoved his hand in his pocket and thrust ten dollars into my hand. "Take this anyway. You may need it. You can send it back any time. And don't forget, Hutch is a right guy. Tell him everything. He's going to be interested. Don't forget to give our love to Eleanor and don't quit now." That was the last time I saw Tip. We wrote him a few letters and returned the money.

It must have been about three-thirty Sunday afternoon when I arrived in Lethbridge and went to Hutch's room. I was feeling very dull, the sort of tiredness that was more mental than physical and prevented me from summoning any enthusiasm. Yet there was no restraint or tension between us. Hutch poured me a drink. It was the one thing I needed. He poured me another and got me talking. I had made up my mind to answer routine questions, leave out the details and refrain from any attempt to build up the adventure and romance that Eleanor and I had enjoyed until now. But Hutch was more than a bank manager. He

91

was the kind of man that helped make the West, one of the old school though young in years. Before I knew it I had told him where I had been in the R.C.M.P., the years during the war, all about Eleanor, the first job, the drive, Harry Hargrave, Joe Gilchrist and all the rest. I answered so many questions my head was spinning, but we had a lot of laughs. If anyone was going to pull me out of this slump Hutch was the man to do it.

"Well, what do you think?" I said finally. "Should we put our tails between our legs and crawl back where we came from—or should we stick?"

"Meet me in the morning around nine-thirty," he said. "We are still building the new bank and I'll be down there getting in the road. The two of us will call on the V.L.A."

In the morning I was slightly hung over and nervous as we climbed the stairs. Mr. Miller was in his office and I introduced Hutch. The bank manager waved his hand and said we were all fixed up to buy the cattle in a way that would be acceptable to the Government. Mr. Miller was relieved and asked for it in writing. Hutch wrote out a statement to that effect. Mr. Miller said he would send it all in to Edmonton and would try to rush things through. When he received clearance he would telephone me to meet him in Pincher Creek.

Back in the new building, amid ladders, workmen and blue prints, I asked Hutch if he wanted me to sign anything. He suggested we wait until we found out what was going to happen. We shook hands on that and I left for the jeep. I started the engine, then shut it off. Had we covered everything? All the Government had was Hutch's statement.

What if they decided to write again asking precisely where the cattle were and for a new report on our finances? This would consume more time but we couldn't put the boots to the Government to hurry them up, and if the Offer to Sell expired, and there were only a few weeks left, nothing could save us. Tip had said: "Don't quit now."

If there was going to be any more fighting I should look up an Irishman. And I knew one in town, the fighting kind, Arthur Beaumont, K.C. He had been police magistrate and before the war we used to meet frequently for dinner and bridge. In addition to his hilarious accounts of exploits during World War I and his early years in Canada afterwards, I remembered his great willingness to drop everything and throw himself into a fight for poor, unfortunate, helpless little people. Perhaps he would like to hear our story!

"Bejasus!" he said when I told it to him. "We've got to move quickly. Why didn't you look me up before this started? I want to meet this bank manager and we are going to see Miller. Then you are going to take me up to the ranch." He cancelled his appointments and I raced down the street after him. "I'm going to do all the talking," he said. "I'm Southern Commander of the Canadian Legion. During the war I helped the Government draw up some of these regulations and I'm going to threaten the whole weight of the Legion behind me if there is any funny business."

He talked to Hutch privately, told me afterwards he knew enough about banking laws to feel Hutch was sticking his neck out. Hutch said he realized this but hadn't the heart to turn me away. Beaumont told him he was my lawyer now

93

and promised to dig up a better plan for both of us. Hutch remembered Tip's and Augie's promises to back any notes but the lawyer wanted a firmer business and legal foundation.

He stormed into the V.L.A. shouting, "Where's the bloody S.S.B.?" (After World War I the V.L.A. was known as the Soldiers' Settlement Board.) I cannot remember what he said except that he was going out to the ranch and that he and the Canadian Legion were very much interested in the case. On the way to the jeep I spotted Harold Haugen on the street. He explained that he had left the Deer Creek and was looking around. I asked him if he would like to visit us for a while and agreed to meet him when I returned with Beaumont.

The indignant Irishman had jumped in with both feet without knowing a fraction of the details. I had talked and explained so much to Augie and Tip and Hutch the previous day that I was trying for short-cuts in my narrative. Beaumont became more puzzled as we progressed because I was talking in chunks, with no sequence, and not helping him much. He was perplexed over the reason for the drive to Medicine Hat, why the cattle deal with Rhodes should fall through, when I remembered to tell him about the silent partners. During the last five miles of the drive he suddenly said: "For the first time I'm beginning to see daylight. I'm getting the picture now. But why go to Medicine Hat and other people after starting up with the silent partners? Keep all your eggs in one basket, boy. Don't try to complicate things."

Arriving at the ranch he met Eleanor at the cabin, said that he was spending the night, the camp cot would be perfect, he loved strong tea any time, and his idea of luxury was to sit by the oven door "measling his shins and sipping tay." He had Eleanor laughing so that she forgot to ask how things were going. Before settling down, however, he said to me: "Take me over to the main house to meet the owner. I'll do the talking and don't interrupt me. I'm going to tell them things that will surprise you." He certainly did. Apparently he was our lawyer and had a large trust account of mine. Everything was going through as originally agreed upon, including the purchase of thirty cows with calves to be picked from the herd now on the place and they were to be paid for in three annual instalments, without interest charges, commencing one year from the sale of the ranch. When Rhodes protested that he had no guarantee and once my brand was on the animals he had no come-back, Beaumont said he would produce a guarantee from the bank to pay each instalment on time whether or not I had the money and that this guarantee would satisfy his lawyers. He added that we had the money to pay for them but everyone was going to stick to the original agreement, verbal or written, all the way down the line.

He returned to the cabin rubbing his hands, proceeded to entertain us hilariously during the evening, drinking strong tea and "measling his shins". Eleanor saw to that. The next day he attended to details we never realized existed, beat up our flagging hopes with Celtic zeal and worked so many miracles we dubbed him the Wizard of Oz. When he left he took with him all our headaches.

On the drive back to Lethbridge he said: "Boy, you found a gold mine." I told him about Harold coming up to visit, said we had so many commitments now we had better take out some insurance against our lack of experience by trying

95

to hire Harold for a year anyway. He thought it was a good idea. Because I couldn't pay wages I asked him if he would draw up a contract later, when all the trouble was over, offering Harold a percentage of the net income.

The Wizard then told me he would be in Calgary by the end of the week and would check the titles of the land. He told us to go ahead and work the ranch as though it was ours.

We did just that. Harold returned with me. It was July and we were late getting started with the haying. We seemed to be working day and night. We had to borrow a team of horses here, hay forks there, and all the neighbours began to rally around. Rhodes would not let us use any equipment until the purchase of the ranch was completed. It gave us a fine chance to discover how good the neighbours really were. And it was fun.

The only cloud appeared in a letter from the V.L.A. with a legal form to be signed by ourselves and the silent partners. It was an undertaking that we were not to pay them in money or kind until we had discharged our debt to the Government. Beaumont said it was a "low blow" but we had no choice except to bother those good people, and I mailed it to them with an apologetic letter. They returned it with the cheery notation that we could get the Government out of the way first and let them be real partners!

At the end of July, 1947, Rhodes returned from town. He came over to the cabin in the evening to tell me he had signed all the papers. Everything had been completed, but his lawyer wanted to see me. He did not know what it was for, but it was important that I do so. We were very busy, so I drove to town early, hoping to return for the best part of the day, and was waiting for the lawyer when he arrived at the office. He was very apologetic, said all the documents were drawn up and that he wanted to see the deal go through quickly. But three more conditions had been imposed. I had to sign an additional legal paper, agreeing to the conditions set forth before the papers could be sent to my lawyers. Those were the instructions from his client. The conditions were as follows: 1. Cash for the cattle (There's that knife again!). 2. Possession of the house until November 15. 3. The right to keep all their possessions on the place until April, 1948, and full use of the cabin.

The lawyer asked me to sign. I shook my head. He wanted to know what I intended to do. I said I would telephone my lawyer and let him know.

When I explained the new conditions to the anxious Irishman I had to hold the receiver a foot away from my ear. He shouted that I was not to sign anything or mention the matter to anyone but to tell the lawyer he would be along the next day. He asked me to meet the bus.

I went back and put in a pretty good day at the ranch. But Eleanor was worried. I told her the Wizard was coming out and he was planning to remain a couple of days. Our cabin had one bedroom, a kitchen and a small pantry. Eleanor, Dane, Timmy and I slept in the bedroom, and Harold in the kitchen on my Air Force camp cot. Harold offered to sleep on the mattress placed on the floor so Beaumont could have the cot.

After the Wizard dismounted from the bus he called on the lawyer and asked him to come along. We drove to the ranch. Beaumont was magnificent. He talked to everyone like a Dutch uncle with a brogue. When he had finished all were eager to return to the original conditions. He gained possession of the papers and I drove him to Lethbridge Sunday evening to spend the night at his home.

Monday morning early we called on Mr. Miller. Beaumont gave him an account of the latest tactics and threatened to sue for everything. He said we simply had to get the final okay from Edmonton before something else turned up. Beaumont wasn't fooling when he threatened to sue, but he didn't want any time to slip by for the effects of his warning to wear off. Mr. Miller admitted he had been worried the last few weeks by the delay in Edmonton. He didn't know as we were talking that things were happening at that very moment.

The clerk who checked the mail came rushing into his office and put down the last piece of red tape—final authority for Miller to close the deal! There it was on his desk and he beamed at us in triumph. It could not have been more timely. Heaving a sigh of relief Beaumont asked: "Can you finish this today?"

Miller said he would telephone Rhodes' lawyers and have all the principals meet in Pincher Creek that afternoon. He asked me to give him time to clear his desk and I walked out with Beaumont. As he turned to go to Court he wagged a finger at me: "Don't sign any papers but the ones Mr. Miller hands you." I grinned back at the genial Irishman and promised.

Then I walked around the streets in a daze. The business had been so long drawn out, and yet it had ended so suddenly. I don't know just where I went but I remember fighting down an urge to stop citizens on the street to tell them the news. Finding myself down at the railway station

I sent off a vague telegram to Eleanor, not realizing that she could not begin to guess the drama was approaching the closing scene. "Bringing home the bacon. Love", I wrote. The date was July 28, 1947.

Then I drove to Pincher Creek as Miller was following in his own car. When he arrived we assembled in the lawyer's office. I had a mad impulse to ask them to hold everything until I fetched Eleanor from the ranch so that she could witness the last chapter in the struggle. We finished signing all the papers at seven o'clock that evening.

It was too bad I couldn't borrow an airplane to shoot up the ranch. I pushed the jeep hard, expecting to find Eleanor tip-toe with excitement. Her calmness infuriated me. Wasn't this a wonderful climax? Wasn't what wonderful? I found that my telegram had left her completely in a fog about developments. She thought I had bought a couple of weaner pigs! Bringing home the bacon, to be sure. What a gal!

Chapter Nine

HAROLD decided to remain with us on a yearly contract and we were soon immersed in long days of heavy work, trying to catch up on lost time. So many fine days and precious hours had been spent running around the country pulling irons out of the fire we had to let everything else wait for the urgency of saving our hay. We had a team and rack, two hay forks, a mower and rake. Because we could not afford any breakdowns caused by my inexperience, Harold ran the mower. We worked around the clock, from five in the morning until ten at night. It was a real struggle to get out of boots and blue jeans in the evening before falling to sleep. In spite of hot weather, nose flies bothering the team and bull dogs attacking man and beast, we kept at it. We forked the hay on the rack, built large loads, hauled to the stack yards and forked the hay off. We built the stacks as high as we could pitch hay. But the method was too old-fashioned and slow. It looked as though we would be working at it until the first snow storm. In the past Mr. Rhodes had put up hay in this fashion but he had used several teams and many men. More progressive outfits had long since been using stackers and sweeps run by horses or tractors. Harold explained the various methods and advised getting a stacker. Mr. Beaumont had made sure we would have a few hundred dollars in the bank for emergencies, so Eleanor and I debated if a stacker could be so classified.

One evening I drove to a neighbour's place to buy Eleanor a present to celebrate the completion of the deal. I returned with six ducks which we launched with appropriate ceremony in the large stock dam in front of the house. I also brought news of an auction sale south of Pincher Creek. A farmer was selling out. Sometimes at these sales a man can pick up a piece of machinery very cheaply if he keeps his head, and this one advertised two home-made sets of stackers and sweeps for horses.

During July, between crises, we had attended a local sale just over the hill about two miles from our place and had wonderful luck. We had purchased a young saddle horse for $20, a bench and some pails for $1.50 and a fair kitchen stove. This was our first experience of a farm auction sale and we were elated with the results. We found out later that the Bougerolle brothers, our neighbours to the west, had wanted the saddle horse and had, in fact, started to bid. But when they noticed me bidding they had stopped. They had heard we were running into tough luck and figured we needed the horse. Heady with the success of buying a horse so cheaply and badly needing a stove, I started to bid on the one in the cabin. A man north of us also started to bid lively. We were the only two interested. When he saw it was the new people who wanted that stove he walked out the door and left me to bid alone. We got it for $8.50.

101

Remembering how well that first auction had turned out for us we decided to try for a stacker to speed up the haying. Harold and I arrived early for the sale and spent an hour looking at all the machinery on display. The stackers were made of logs and heavy bridge timbers; it looked as though moving one would be a big engineering job. We debated the feasibility of taking it apart, moving the sections and rebuilding at home. But the more we sized up the contraption the less we liked the idea. As the sale progressed from household effects to animals and tool and harness, winding up with the big machinery, I asked other men for their views on the possibility of moving one of the heavy stackers. One chap told me he had a 'slide overshot' horse stacker and sweep, factory built, at his farm much closer to our home which he would sell for $100. He had just bought a tractor outfit. He would also lend us a strong trailer our jeep could handle for hauling the outfit home. I spoke to Harold, and as he thought it well worth looking at we arranged to stop in after the sale. We spent the rest of the day there watching other men buy at reasonable prices tools and machinery we could well have used but felt we could do without for the time being. If we were going to lose no time improving the hay land, however, we would need a plough, so I told Harold to bid if he thought there was a bargain. At the end of the sale he slipped in a quick bid for an old sulky plough with good shares. Such ploughs were so out of date in this rich and modern district we got it for $2.50. It was the kind used by the early homesteaders to break the land. Flushed with success we bid again on a binder, in good working order with new canvasses and

102

rollers. It was knocked down to us for $9.50. When someone told us a new canvas cost $8.00 we felt even better.

On the way home we looked at the factory-built stacker and sweep, decided to buy and arranged to pick them up next day. Now we really began to make time with the haying. Harold ran the horse sweep while I raised the sweep load on the stacker with the jeep. Then I built the stack while he was out getting the next load. We put up our first big high stack in five hours. Using the old method we had discarded, handling the hay twice as much and damaging the leaves, it would have taken us three days or better to put the same amount of hay in a number of smaller stacks. It was hot and heavy work for the stacker, but it was child's play when compared with the old time-consuming system. We began to catch up and think of other things besides hay. I recalled the words of an old timer who had cautioned: "City folks holler for a forty-hour week and I figger a man in the country is entitled to a day off. Don't you folks get in the habit of working Sundays. It's all right for an emergency but I did it for years and I know it's a bad habit to break." We decided to try taking a day off.

The valley between our end of the Porcupine Hills and the Livingstone Range of the Rockies is called the North Fork. That is the North Fork of the Old Man River whose headwaters come rushing out of the mountains through the breath-taking gap about thirty miles from our place. If you climb our hill to the west you can follow the whole lovely valley for miles north and south with the naked eye. Directly across, so massive and close you feel like reaching out to touch it, is the Livingstone Range. A great many of the

103

early settlers who came out from England chose this valley and from a scenic point of view I think it was a fair exchange. Some had money, built fine homes and imported good horses and stock. Others started by homesteading. But all were sportsmen and in those free and easy days they played a lot of polo. They also built almost sixty years ago a tiny log church, known today as the Livingstone Church, which is part of the Foothills Mission. This church is about fourteen miles from us and during the summer, weather permitting, a service is held the first Sunday in the month. Mrs. Mowat, the wife of George Mowat, our closest neighbour on the north, who had left a desk in London about forty-five years ago and settled in the North Fork, telephoned Eleanor to ask if we would care to attend the service in August. We thought it would be a nice thing to do in the calm and peace that had descended upon us after all our adventures.

When this Sunday came it was a lovely day, cool, sunny and clear as though the air had been washed by some gigantic air conditioning unit. All scrubbed and shining and in our best clothes, we drove carefully over Cabin Hill to Mowat's in the open jeep lest we get dusty. Then we transferred to the Mowats' car for the drive to church. Here we were, going to church with our neighbours in our own community. We were going to meet many of the old-timers and their descendants. It gave us a warm feeling, a fresh reminder that we actually belonged after so much wandering.

Mr. Mowat described the early settlers, the young Englishmen who came out for adventure bringing their polo with them. His own brother had followed him out to become the Anglican Vicar in the Foothills Mission. As this was to be a special service we were to meet a larger number than would normally attend. Some of the young people were to be confirmed. The Bishop of Calgary was expected. We found the little church standing all by itself in the middle of a field, with hitching posts and stables adjoining. People were arriving in cars and trucks, in wagons and by saddle horse, dressed in their Sunday best. Mrs. Mowat took Eleanor around to introduce her to the ladies while George had me meet some of the men. There was 'Posthole' Smith. The nickname had been picked up in the early days and Posthole was proud of it. It had to appear that way in the social column of the Pincher Creek *Echo* or people wouldn't know which Smith was meant. His brother was known as 'Dropper' Smith. There was Harry Gunn who came out in 1890. He had been one of the stars on the famous Cowley polo team which had travelled to Winnipeg and down through the western states. The team had distinguished themselves by winning an international match at Seattle and probably caused many people to wonder where the devil Cowley was located.

We leaned over the hitching post while George reminisced about the early days in his English accent. "We had a lot of fun then," he said. "It was quite a community of old countrymen. Some of them had fine houses where they gave very correct and magnificent parties. Everyone was invited whether you were struggling on a quarter section of land or managing a big place. It was a joke to see the well dressed men from the Saturday ball at work the following week. In those days we had two outfits—greasy old cowboy clothes and our white ties and tails. This little church was always well attended on Sunday. Everyone would ride or travel by buckboard to the service very sedately. But as soon as church was over they would gallop and whoop their way in a mad race to the river bottom where they played polo the rest of the day.

"I will never forget one lady just out from England to visit the Kemmis or Sandemann ranch—you know, the Sandemann wine people. She was alone in the house when she answered a knock at the back door. It rather horrified her to see a run-down Englishman with a good accent peddling meat. His hands and arms and shirt front were all bloody. He had just killed a beef, and as he couldn't keep it all on his bachelor establishment he was riding around to the neighbours to sell the surplus. The lady thought this man had quite come down in the world. When they took her to church on Sunday and then to the polo in the afternoon, she admired the very handsome person in immaculate white riding breeches and polished boots, well mounted, who was captain of the winning team. But when she was taken up to be introduced she was horrified to learn he was 'the butcher' who had called a few days previously. It was a good joke for quite a while."

I kept thinking of the old days as George had described them when we entered the church. It was a typical rural service such as one could expect in a church used once a month during the summer. Someone was hammering up a curtain and the Ladies' Aid were putting last minute touches to the flowers while the bishop hovered discreetly in the doorway. But it was a lovely service. For us it was Thanksgiving. As I looked around at these pleasant faces I couldn't help thinking that although the old days of polo and fancy parties were over the same kind of people were here, living the life that had been created by hope and fortitude so many years ago.

After the service the whole congregation was invited to a buffet supper on the lawn of the Lynch-Staunton ranch where all sorts of nice people came up to say hello and welcome us. As we drove back with the Mowats the worry of the preceding months began to fade as though it had been a bad dream. Our plans, formed in another kind of life, were actually taking shape. We were finding security. Peace was in the valley, contentment in the hills. Here was a new life to be developed; the main risk was over. We only had to prove ourselves with these new friends. Eleanor and I held hands. We didn't have to talk. Timmy was asleep in his basket and Dane was barely hanging on to consciousness. It was ten o'clock when we got home. The ranch looked different. It had taken on new stature. We had arrived in our spiritual home.

A letter from the Provincial Government sent me off to town. They had approved a brand for us. In years to come, after it had been established and handed down to our sons, the brand would be as well known as our own name. I had the blacksmith make us the branding irons—the Seven, the C and the Bar. As I threw them in the jeep for the trip back I felt they would complete the cycle. We had the ranch, and when we put our brand on the cattle it would really interpret for us the true meaning of the mysterious mass of legal documents and deeds I had signed.

The Rhodes were still in the main house, so I went over to fix a day for the branding. We decided to stage it on Sunday. We would need a crew of five or six, and Eleanor had to plan on two meals, served in relays in the cabin. Needing a good roper we decided to ask Fred Hewitt, an old time cowboy who had worked on the big Walronde outfit and had travelled in the Welsh Brothers rodeo down East one or two seasons before settling down on his own place. I drove over to ask Fred, whose ranch was just beyond Mowat's. Then I got word to Jim Carney, at whose place we had bought the ducks. Mr. Rhodes said he would get hold of a few others.

In addition to the roper there must be a man to tend the branding fire and hand the irons through the corrals to the man branding. A couple of husky lads are required to wrestle the calves, one with a leg lock on the head, the other stretched out behind the calf to secure the hind legs. You need a good man to mark the ear and castrate, and one to check the horns, dehorning with knife and caustic or dehorning paste. I had to purchase a vaccine gun with spare needles and a fresh supply of vaccine for blackleg and malignant edema. Each calf had to be vaccinated at the same time as it was branded. Normally these operations would be completed much earlier in the calf's life, often in two stages, before the end of June. But here it was August, in fly time and hot. The calves were just that much larger and stronger and we figured the 'rasslers' would have to spell each other off.

We had everything assembled before Saturday but Eleanor's job really started then. She had to plan large meals, make a number of pies, have everything ready by Saturday night. We insisted she had to attend the branding and take pictures, so she decided on baking a huge ham the day before.

It was almost time for evening chores on Saturday. I had just checked the supply of wood for the branding fire, assembled shovel and crow-bar for the pit, collected branding irons and lariats, looked over the roping corral and the chute when I noticed trouble by the blacksmith shop. The pigs were out! We had recently purchased two little weaners and had fenced them in by the pig house until they became accustomed to their new home.

I ran towards them, calling to Eleanor for help. We had to keep them together and try to drive or entice them back into their quarters. Eleanor came running. We knocked down the little fence, got them corralled without stirring them up, and together nailed everything back into place. I walked back with Eleanor to the cabin for the milk pails while she explained that her preparations were completed. Poor Eleanor! . . . The sight that greeted her at the cabin was heart-breaking. Her lovely ham that had been left cooling on the table had been dragged outside by the dog and partly eaten. Fortunately for the culprit we couldn't lay our hands on him at that moment. Eleanor lamented tearfully that now she wouldn't be able to watch the branding but would have to spend the day standing over the stove. And we should have to serve stringy pieces of beef instead of tender slices of ham.

We awoke to a lovely calm day, were out at five to do up the chores in mounting excitement. Mr. Rhodes and I were to remain at the corrals. Harold was to take a couple of riders to round up the herd in the summer range, and while his helpers held the cattle in a bunch Harold was to cut out the cows with calves he selected for our basic herd. Then he had to drive them through the gate into the horse pasture which leads down to the corrals. They hoped to get going early, before the heat of the day and the flies should stir up the critters and make them balky. As Harold started up the horse pasture he met Jim Carney riding down and together they disappeared from sight.

Down to the corrals I hauled a pail of hot water smelling strongly of disinfectant, the vaccine, syringe and needles—all the paraphernalia we would need. Fred arrived and we squatted on our heels before the fire pit talking cow and hay crop. Henry Neufeld walked over from his ranch on the east boundary. I wanted to start the fire and begin heating the irons but Fred said: "Plenty of time. The irons will get hot enough between the time the herd is corralled and we get the cows cut back." So we twisted smokes and waited. I wanted to be everywhere at once—out riding with Harold and at the same time checking things at the corral. But we just waited.

About nine o'clock we could see cattle and horsemen milling around at the top of the horse pasture. I wanted to get busy right away. But Fred just said: "Plenty of time yet. They are going to be quite a while getting the right calves with the cows they want." Indeed, it was quite a job and I didn't realize until a year later how difficult it is to ensure you have them properly paired.

By eleven they were starting down the pasture and we

110

disappeared out of sight, leaving the main gate wide open. The cows were suspicious and did not cooperate in taking their calves away from their playground. Once inside the main gate they had to be moved into the smaller roping corral, and then the cows cut back. Here the matrons pressed up against the little corral, bawling at their calves and the little ones answering so continuously it was difficult to hear or understand what anyone was saying.

As soon as the irons were almost red hot, the syringe tested and filled with vaccine, the boys checked each other for jobs and positions. Then the boss nodded and said: "Let's go."

Fred rode into the corral, shaking out his loop, and hind-footed a calf. As the little animal ran out full length on the rope, bucking and plunging, it was dragged over to the side where the irons were waiting. The wrestlers sometimes used an extra rope to secure the head, and by pulling tail and foot rope on opposite sides they upset the calf. Then they would dive for head and hind legs, stretching it on the correct side. If a head rope wasn't used it took a good man to grab the calf by flank and neck, lift the animal and slam it to the ground. Quickly Harold approached with the first iron and after brushing the hide clean of dirt pressed on the 7. Back to the fire to exchange his 7 for the C and on it would go, the C for the Bar—and he was through. At the same time Jim had his knife and disinfectant at work if the calf was a bull, turning it into a steer. Another man was at the head, cutting the horn button and rubbing in caustic, while yet another was shooting into the neck or shoulder 5 c.c.'s of vaccine. As each man finished his job he stood

111

clear to replenish his supply of vaccine, check tools, clean knife or coil a spare rope out of the way. A tally man marked up the score, divided into steers and heifers. When all the jobs had been checked the wrestlers jumped clear and the roper went after another calf.

As the hot day wore on we changed jobs around and it turned into a sporting event with the interest mainly on the roping. We tried roping on foot, and after dabbing the loop correctly took a couple of quick turns on the snubbing post in the centre. Men were leaping and racing out of the way as the calf usually raced around the corral, winding up on the snubbing post before it could be stopped. Another rope on head and one forefoot, so the animal would not choke, stretched to one side of the corral, made it easier to handle the larger, more energetic calves. It was easy to get tripped or knocked about. Rope burns and bruises from the hind foot of a protesting calf made their appearance on legs, arms, shoulders, even necks.

It was a tired, hot and dusty crew that finished the last calf. We walked up to the cabin for our dinner, some of us limping from bruises. In the shade of the cabin there was beer in a wash tub full of cold water from the well. It tasted like champagne. We ate heartily in spite of the heat. The job was half finished. The cows had to be run through the chute and branded in a primitive type of squeeze. At last it was completed, and Fred Hewitt put the final word to an active, exciting and satisfying day. "Well, Gray, now you are in the cattle business." I looked at his new car and his well dressed wife and children, thought of his comfortable little home over the hills as he added:

112

"Everything I got out of this world was provided by those Herefords. Just hang on to the old cow's tail, boy, and she'll pull you out of your troubles."

These were our first cattle, as nice a little bunch of cows as any man would want to start with. When everyone had left Eleanor and I strolled down to the corrals in the cool of the evening and looked at each animal before turning it into the bull pasture to be kept separate from the Rhodes' herd. We took a long look at the brand, 7C—on the right hip. Not one calf looked ill or as though it had suffered more than momentary anguish. Eleanor had taken some snapshots and wondered if the brand would show up. There were thirty cows with their calves at $125 each pair. And we had bought one of the bulls for $200. That made it $3,950 worth of stock in the corral. A year from now we would have to make the first of three annual payments for them. Would we be able to keep the calves until they were long yearlings, and could we get hold of more cattle to run on shares? Would the price of beef go down suddenly and sharply, forcing us to sell the whole herd? If it held steady and if we could pick up more cattle either on shares or by running them at so much a head per month, we might scrape through, selling the calves out of the cows and holding the thirty head of matrons in our herd. It was going to take us a long time to build up. Rhodes used to run around one hundred and fifty cows! I'll bet some of the neighbours must have wondered this day if we were going to make it with only thirty cows for a start. I could see now what the V.L.A. Board meant when they insisted on our having a herd first.

Eleanor must have sensed my thoughts. We turned the thirsty animals out to water and grass, then walked up the valley until we were standing on a knoll looking down at the buildings, corrals and strip farms in the distance. "I hope our branding parties will be bigger and better in future, old thing," I said, "and that you will be out there with us all day taking part in the fun."

"Remember what Fred told you," she replied. "You're in the cattle business now. All we have to do is hang on to their tails and they will pull us through."

I wondered. Would Fred start out like this today?

Chapter Ten

THIS is a great country for winter wheat. With a reasonable winter wheat seeded in the fall gets a better start than spring wheat and the farmers are able to harvest it ahead of the early frosts. By this time everyone with winter wheat was busy cutting his crops. We remembered Jim Carney who had lent us a team of horses and a set of harness for our haying and also helped us brand. Harold and I decided to keep on the right side of the ledger and when we heard Jim was about to stook his grain we went over there for two days. I had never done this sort of work before and was dismayed to see the long rows of bundles lying on the strips. We worked without forks, which means more bending, and Harold set a terrific pace which almost played out the rest of us. We finished the stooking in two days but it nearly wrecked me. The Carneys were very grateful. It was the largest crop they had cut in years.

We had just settled down at home again when Angus Maufort, our neighbour to the south, paid us a call. George Mowat was behind with his haying. His best hay had been lying in cocks on the home place. Angus explained that George had suffered a bad accident some years before that had slowed him down and he wondered if the three of us could go over there and give George a day. We left next morning with a team and wagon and three strong backs to put up most of the field. We forked the hay into wagons by hand but George and his hired man operated a stacker to take off the loads. After sizing us up on this job Angus wondered if we could help him for two days to get his clover bundles stacked. He offered to pay us going wages. We couldn't continue working for good will, so I made a counter proposition. Angus kept pigs and I wondered if he would trade us a finished pig for our work. He thought that was a fine arrangement and for our part we needed meat for the winter. A pig would help. So we moved down there with team and wagon. Harold did the stacking, being an artist at building bundle stacks, while Angus and I spent two days hauling loads of bundles to him. I began learning how to pitch bundles. The lessons were credited towards the precious pig.

Rhodes finally left the main house and when we returned from working out I thought all we had to do was move our things over. But Eleanor took us on an inspection tour and laid down the law. Left for us was an old bed, some shelves in the pantry and the linoleum on the kitchen floor—we had bought that. Eleanor began pulling paper off the walls, showing us layer after layer of old wall paper underneath. She took us to the bedrooms and made us look at greasy finger marks on woodwork and walls. She made us inspect the floors, she pulled up the linoleum, and when she finished talking we realized we would be lucky to get in there before the end of September.

While we spent a few days fixing fences Eleanor dusted and swept the house. Then with a knife she scraped the woodwork. When she had removed the old dirt she put on rubber gloves and with plenty of lye in the water scrubbed the floors. Then she painted walls and ceilings and woodwork after papering some of the rooms with a strong building paper that would take a cheap casein paint. Her first complete success was with the little boys' room which she transformed into a bright cheery place. After scrubbing, painting and waxing the floor she closed up the room before tackling the next job.

It was no place for a man, so we cleared out. Eleanor suggested that if we were out of the way and she didn't have to plan meals for us she would make better time. As Carneys were about to start threshing we joined their outfit for three days. They paid eight dollars a day for a team and wagon, six dollars for a man. I let Harold take the team as I didn't know how a threshing crew worked, and found myself the field pitcher. If you have a team and wagon you throw on your load with the help of the field pitcher, rest while you drive in to the machine, then pitch off the load. Then you rest while the team takes you out to the field where the field pitcher helps you load again. I was the field pitcher. There wasn't any rest for me. In fact, I could hardly keep up with the six teams that kept coming at me with horrible regularity. Thank heaven it lasted only three days. We slept at home, stumbling around in the dark to do our own chores, downing a hasty breakfast and rushing by jeep to get on the crew by daylight. As the outfit travels from one farm to the next the wives go along to help the next neighbour with the meals, and the women vie with

117

one another to provide the best grub. The tables literally groan with the food and I have never eaten better than on a threshing crew. At night we would return home, utterly fagged out, to find that our milk cows had strayed and in spite of complaining muscles we had to search for them in the dark.

After finishing the three days in that outfit I would have been content to rest on my laurels. But when we returned home with our team and wagon Eleanor announced there were two calls for us. Angus wanted to know if Harold could take his place on the Dumont crew and Gus Dingreville wanted to know if we could come down there. Working for Angus would help to buy that pig. If Harold joined his crew I would have to show up at Dingreville's. Harold left at noon with team and wagon next day to put in ten days. I spent another day hauling and splitting fire wood for Eleanor, then went off for a week of threshing. Harold slept with the crew this time but I had to hop nimbly back and forth by jeep to keep up with the chores at home. This time, though, I played it smart. I grabbed a wagon. They could catch some other dude for field pitcher. We needed the money. And as in all hard jobs I found the body quickly toughened up to it so that each day I had more bounce.

But, thank goodness, the work came to an end. Being with the Dingreville crew was fun but our own place needed attention. Back home we got out the bargain binder. In the spring we had hurriedly seeded a field of thirty acres to oats. Being without a seeder we had followed the old biblical custom of seeding by hand. Now the oats were maturing rapidly. When Harold first inspected the field he wondered just how it had been seeded, the pattern was so peculiar.

Now we had to test the binder. While Harold checked and assembled the parts I went over the machine with an oil can as I had watched it done at Carney's. When all was ready we intended to pull it with the jeep and try it around the edge of the field. With Harold on the seat working the levers I drove around in low tractor gear. It worked beautifully until at the first corner the platform bit into the earth, breaking two slats. Slowly we returned to the blacksmith shop. Eleanor noticed our return but was so afraid things were not going well didn't let on she saw us. Quickly we replaced the slats, raised the hitch and were off again. Now Eleanor appeared from hiding to wave, so we stopped to insist that she come out with us and see it working. She protested that there was bread rising on the stove but we were firm about it, so carrying Timmy she got into the jeep with me. Dane jumped on the back and we climbed the hill to the oat field again. We must have looked a queer crew—Timmy gurgling happily on Eleanor's knee, the rest of us shouting and pointing as Harold put the machine in gear, manipulating the levers furiously. Everyone was excited and happy that it should work. We cut all around the edge of the field for feed. The trial decided Harold that the oats would not be ready for another week. But the machine worked; it hardly missed tying a bundle. Harold had to make only minor adjustments. Indeed, it was a very good buy.

Before we could cut our oats, however, an early mid-September storm hit the country, knocking the grain flat with heavy, wet snow. We were building a new fence around the house at the time and thought of our cattle still on the summer grass. As we had fenced our haystacks up

119

north it was clearly time to move them to winter grass. As Mr. Rhodes had taken his saddle horse away and we had only tried the young twenty-dollar horse once, Harold and I set out on foot. We found most of the cattle bunched together out of the wind on a steep side-hill where we could work them along a fence line to a gate in a corner. Some had broken through the fence already but most of them were standing dejectedly in a sullen group. We slithered and crawled our way up the slope, Harold cutting off at an angle to move the few head already through the fence along with the main bunch. Just as he disappeared over the top I flushed a little black bear cub just ahead of me, higher up among some rocks. He scampered like mad over the top in line with Harold and I wondered how the two of them would react at the meeting. As the little ball of fur disappeared I thought it was going to run between Harold's legs. Harold told me later the bear must have thought he was surrounded as he tried to go several ways at once!

We moved the cattle without trouble and returned to the house. That was a mistake. Eleanor decided she could put us to work. She had one room left—the kitchen. We stripped all the paper off the walls, pulled thousands of tacks, swept the walls and ceiling of an accumulation of dead flies and dust and rolled up the linoleum for scrubbing. Eleanor figured that after applying hot water, soap and elbow grease to the floor and walls and re-laying the linoleum over the entire floor we could move in. Papering the walls and ceiling could be postponed until winter when we could help more easily. At any rate we should enter a clean house —she was sure of that. After some sandwiches and tea Harold went out to try the new horse while Eleanor and

I finished the kitchen. Another day of scrubbing and it would be over. Then we could really unpack—for the first and last time, we hoped. It had been a tough month for Eleanor, working hard and fitting in with our comings and goings, but she was delighted with results.

We moved at the end of September, on Eleanor's birthday. Her comment was: "What better birthday present could I ask?" After being in that tiny cabin so long, four of us in the bedroom, Harold in the kitchen, with very little privacy and no elbow room, we could now spread ourselves through six rooms. We didn't have furniture but we had the rooms and enough beds to go around. There was a kitchen table and five plain chairs. My old saddle box and camp cot now served for extra seats. Once in a while we would look in the mail order catalogues at the sumptuous beds with spring mattresses, the chesterfields and easy chairs and think that some day, if we held on to the cow's tail long enough, we could certainly improve our living conditions. In the meantime wasn't it enough to think we had the ranch and thirty cows with calves? Of course, they weren't paid for, but we were on the way. We had been kept too busy to worry about beef prices or to work out figures on paper estimating our margin between safety and disaster. We knew one thing for sure. We were still strong and healthy. The things we could see and touch were in our name, and the work we had done threshing, the heavy, muscle-screaming work, was going to help feed us through the winter. Moreover, Harold and I had $96 coming to us. If there was a pinch later one of us could always go out and work. We had an enormous potato crop and a fine garden.

We were making our own butter and had our own hens producing eggs. No, we wouldn't be hungry.

When the snow disappeared we were blessed with lovely Indian summer. The hills donned their red and yellow and brown garments. The wood smoke from our fires hung lazily in the air. We dug up garden produce, storing it in bins down in the cellar. Indian summer is almost as thrilling a time to be alive as it is in the spring when everything is greening up.

When Eleanor was alone one day an Indian arrived, the first to visit. She wondered how to handle him as she watched him tie his horse to the hitching post and shuffle up the walk. It was Jim Crowflag, a minor chief of the Piegans. The timber limits of their reserve border our north fence. Jim is quite tall for an Indian, old-fashioned and courtly in manner, with long braided hair tied with coloured ribbon hanging in two plaits, one over each shoulder. He speaks good English and is very fond of children. Eleanor asked him to stay for a meal and he spent the time questioning her about England and the life there. They got along fine. So did Jim and Dane, who was wide-eyed and slightly awed at the majestic sight of this native aristocrat. Eleanor told us later it was sweet to watch the two of them conversing, Jim so gentle with the little boy. I remember meeting the old Indian in town a year later and his first question was: "How is Dane?" At the end of the meal Eleanor took our cigarette machine, rolled Jim a smoke and presented it to him. It was just the right gesture and Eleanor said you could see the old boy was pleased.

Our relations with the Indians have always been happy. They have never camped on us or taken advantage of any hospitality. Occasionally on a fine Sunday Jim and Bob Crow Eagle will drop by on horseback, stop for tea and a smoke, play with the children on their horses and ride away. Experience with the plains Indians seem to bear out the saying that their religion consists of horses, dogs and children. They generally pack carbines in saddle buckets, for their timber limits abound with game.

A younger Indian also arrived once when Eleanor was alone the first fall but did not have such a prepossessing manner. When he asked for some shells for his gun she gave him what few we had. In telling us about it later Eleanor feared our ridicule but I believed that only time would tell if it would lead to a procession of Indians looking for handouts. He did come back a week later but stopped only long enough to give her a roast of venison. The Indians have never broken faith with us.

When our field of oats was ready for cutting they were so flat the binder was useless without attachments. Gus Dingreville thought of us and offered his set of pick-ups as well as a quiet team to go with our old veterans as we needed four horses on the binder. Angus sent over his set of pick-ups also. With this added equipment Harold started cutting the oats. It was fun working at home, stooking oats of our own for a change. When they had cured sufficiently we had to haul and stack them. While the oats were in the stook we had feed racks to make and the corrals to fix for weaning.

At this time we fell into a couple of nice little deals. Gus had told me one day: "You should have another milk cow for your kids." We were milking 'Shorty', one of the beef type cows bought from Rhodes. I told Gus we had to wait until we could afford it. "No matter the money now," he replied. "I let you have an old Jersey. We got too many cows. You try her out a couple of months and maybe you pay me next year. It no matter." I rode down to look at the animal. She was quite old, due to calf the next March but still in a fair amount of milk. Gus said he would sell her for $75 with all the time to pay I wanted. So I wrote him a demand note and chased the cow home. About the same time the chap who had sold out his small farm that summer called and wanted to know if I would pasture the saddle mare and colt he had left. Since we needed a horse I couldn't charge him pasture. He then offered to let us have another colt out of the mare for her keep. So now we had two horses to ride.

Fred Hewitt had always been good to us, helping with our first branding and some friendly advice. After the branding I told him to be sure and call us if he needed help some day and sure enough he got in touch when it was time to stack his green feed. I rode over on the young horse and joined Fred with three other neighbours. We were working in some well wooded valleys. I was helping Fred with the stacking when one of the men on a wagon called out: "Hey, boys! There are some deer in the next pasture."

Those hill-billies seem to work in the fields with a hunting knife in their belts and a gun handy. The work became a bit disorganized. Someone shoved a gun into my hands and pushed me off with a man I had just met. He was an old hand at deer hunting and we snaked to the top of a small hill on our bellies with our caps turned backwards. I thought he was crazy, for I had watched the deer high-tail it into the woods at right-angles to our course. But he whispered: "They'll swing back around. Get ready for one

124

quick shot when we top this ridge. They won't wait." Sure enough there they were, and we brought a young buck back with us.

It was very dark and snowing heavily when I started for home. I couldn't see the trail through the woods but left it to the horse as we climbed around the edge of Squaw Butte. Into the woods we went and out on the other side to start the descent for home. I had a haunch of venison in a sack over the saddle horn, feeling mighty good from the activity and good fellowship of the day. Through the soft snow haze I could see the cheery warm lantern light slanting on the fresh snow away down below and I could imagine the warm kitchen with the smell of fresh bread and supper on the stove. The horse perked up when he came to our fence and whinnied softly. Eleanor and the boys would be waiting with a big welcome, and I had a surprise for them. I thought it must have been like this in the old days. It was one of the delicious little moments that seem to crop up without warning to convince one that, taking the bad with the good and averaging it all out, it was indeed a very rewarding life.

Harold and I stacked our green feed. We talked a bit about our operations to date. I was sending Hutch, the bank manager in Lethbridge, regular letters and perhaps a too glowing report about our adventures. Now I felt like writing him about trying for a deal on more cattle. We estimated the amount of feed we had stacked and were then putting up. We figured we could handle a couple of carloads of cattle. I wanted to write Augie but sounded Hutch out first so that I could give Augie an alternative. If the bank agreed I could get Augie to buy me some and sign a note at the bank, or if Augie felt like it I could winter some of his. Hutch wrote back with the okay to sound him out. I wrote to Augie in Medicine Hat. He telephoned me from Claresholm, asking if I could get over there next day.

Harold and I rode to Cowley. It was cold and blustery. Then Harold turned around and fogged it for home with the horses. I took a bus to Claresholm, had a meal and spent the evening in the hotel with Augie talking cattle. He asked about our grass, the feed we had put up, what we were running in the way of stock and how we were standing financially. I explained what I had to pay the V.L.A. next year and how much I had to pay off on the cattle we bought from Rhodes. Augie wanted to know what I was paying Harold. When I told him Harold was working on a contract Augie felt we needed a lot more cattle to make it worth while for the boy. But he didn't say what he had in mind that night.

The next day he took me to my first cattle auction. It was quite an education. Individual ranchers were selling more cattle in one lot than we had on the whole ranch and buyers were snapping them up without batting an eye. Augie wasn't interested most of the day, but he slipped in a fast bid and caught a couple of carloads of choice heifers. That evening he remarked casually: "If I was sure they were bred I would let you have them, but they had better go on cover crop."

Then he told me he would send us some big steers, a couple of carloads, early in December. In the meantime, if I could get a truck to meet me at Granum, he would send me back with a load of calves. I tried to find out what the arrangement would be but Augie was vague. He said when he found the steers he would ship them, then write us about a deal. He figured we could make money on steers but until he had bought them he didn't know how the deal would go. I told him that Hutch agreed I could buy anything that seemed reasonable and I was sure I could give him a cheque for the calves. "We'll talk about it in the morning," said Augie. "Just get on the telephone for the truck and tell him to meet us at Granum tomorrow about nine o'clock."

We met the truck and travelled in convoy to a farm. Augie had moved a bunch of cows and calves up from the short grass country around Manyberries and we chased fifteen head of blocky little calves up the chute into the truck. Augie was chuckling as he waved me to the truck and told us to get going. "Don't you want a cheque now?" I asked.

"Pay me when you turn them over," he shouted. "I stole them anyway."

"But how much are they, Augie?"

"Forty dollars each," he replied.

It wasn't so bad buying Dingreville's old Jersey cow for $75. I could make that much threshing. But here I was riding with $600 worth of little dogies. What if some of them should get pneumonia and die? Were we jumping into deals too quickly? All of them on the cuff too. I always had these worries when I went to town. Back on the ranch we never seemed to have time to worry. We were busy all the time, we were happy and the ranch always gave us faith. It wouldn't let us down.

This was Friday. With considerable snow on the highway I didn't think the truck could take the calves right home. At

Cowley 1 telephoned Harold to ride with our horses to Dingreville's. I was sure of getting that far with the truck and we could unload them there and trail them the three miles home.

It was about seven when I reached the Dingreville place. We dumped the calves off into a snow bank. They had just been taken off the cows and we wondered how they would behave. But after some preliminary skirmishing with the horses we got them strung out. We made the last mile home in bright moonlight.

On Saturday we had our first good look at them. They were a fine lot. We put them through the chute and snipped the ends of their tails for identification. Then we rounded up the rest of the herd and drove them into the corral, cut back the cows and had all the calves locked up for weaning. Most ranchers wean in the late fall, the latter part of November or early December. This gives the cow a better chance to come through the winter stronger, have a larger calf in the spring, and the rancher generally feeds the weaners well during the winter to keep them growing. Now it was almost the last week in November.

Sunday morning the weather seemed settled. We decided we could take a chance on branding the new arrivals and at the same time vaccinate all the calves for hemorrhagic septicimia to prevent the danger of pneumonia or diphtheria. Although we had worked around the district by now so that we knew most of the neighbours we had not paired off with any of them to exchange work regularly. We could do with help this day but we rather hesitated to ask anyone. Everyone had been terribly kind in lending us equipment and giving us advice but we felt that in some measure we

128

had paid them all back. Harold had picked up with Marcel Dingreville, the son of Gus, and we thought he could ask Marcel to give us a hand that afternoon. Eleanor volunteered as well. By taking more time to do the job and using several lariats we thought we could get through the work. Branding the new calves would take time but when that was finished it wouldn't take long to run them all through the chute for the vaccinating.

It was the same old thrill all over again but this time it was more fun because of the surprises. We had reckoned without the neighbours. Before we could take all the stuff down to the corral and get the fire going they started to arrive. When we spotted the first sleigh coming up the valley Eleanor began stoking up the fire and mixing a batch of hot biscuits. They crowded into the kitchen and when we pointed to our few inadequate chairs, the boxes and camp cot, they all laughed at our embarrassment. Single riders appeared and Eleanor began to panic at the thought of our six cups and insufficient cutlery. The cowboys in their high heeled boots just squatted on their heels, flicking cigarette ashes into the cuffs of their jeans. The second sleigh load brought the Mowat family, four of them, and as they shook off their wraps they announced cheerfully that they had spotted four more riders coming up the valley! Everyone had another good laugh at our predicament. They seemed to crowd the kitchen so that Eleanor couldn't get organized and you simply could not move around to pass the tea and biscuits. Six families were represented, and three nationalities. I couldn't tell you how many were present but children were swarming everywhere and the only way we might have counted them was through the cattle chutes.

It must have been our house-warming and we didn't know it, or just a great big Porcupine Hill-billie gesture, entirely spontaneous, to let us know we were accepted. No one party seemed to know the other was coming. Finally Bill Lagarde rode up on his famous horse 'Pancake' with a saddle bag full of elk steaks as a present. He had just returned from his annual hunting trip in the mountains. It made a lump in our throats to sense their friendship and kindliness. All the men came out to the corrals for the sport of pitching their skill against the lively calves. We vaccinated forty-five of them. They represented a potential of $5,000 in stock. Of course, here on the ranch I didn't doubt for a second our faith in the future or recall my town worry about buying Augie's calves for $600 on time. We then branded the fifteen in about an hour. Marcel tried to throw one calf alone. It was so heavy he went down with it and they wrestled on the ground. Panting, he turned to me. "Say, fellow, how much did you say these dogies are going to cost you?"

"Forty dollars apiece," I replied.

"You didn't *buy* them—you *stole* them."

We adjourned to the house for more food, scalding tea and good talk. It was a wonderful day to be alive and ranching in the Porcupine Hills.

The first week of weaning is tricky. Day and night you have the cows around bawling continually for their calves and the hungry little ones bawling back. The noise can be heard from the house at all hours. All the gates to the corrals have to be left open or the cows will walk through the fences anyway, and you just have to sit it out patiently until they get used to the idea and move off to graze. When they start drifting off you think it will be quiet in a few hours, but the old cows suddenly remember their calves and come trotting back to take up the chorus again. This reminds the others, so that the noise picks up, dies down, and repeats in waves. That is why you always hope for good weather during weaning. The cows won't eat and drink properly and if a blizzard comes up suddenly it certainly pulls them down.

Fortunately our corrals held for our first weaning. One must also be careful in handling the calves. The new ones had been brought a good many miles in a cold, draughty truck and the vaccine we gave them takes a few weeks to have any effect. Harold practically wrapped them in cotton wool. Alone, I would have shovelled the feed to them and the odd one might have had trouble handling the roughage. But Harold stayed out there from early morning until late at night giving them a little feed at a time to clean up. One calf which developed a cold was put in a barn out of the wind, in a special straw-filled pen we made. It kept its appetite, had warm water and ten c.c.'s of vaccine. We saved it.

Angus rode up one day just at the end of November to have his hair cut. There was a dance at the school that night to raise money for the children's Christmas party. The school is a little over two miles from the house. We had talked previously about going but we had no place to leave the children and disliked the idea of taking them along. Apparently it was the custom, in a country where baby-sitters are as rare as ulcers, to take the whole family to the dances. We were luke-warm about dancing, feeling that we had enjoyed our fling before starting a family and that it would be better not to begin again now. We intended to send our money with Harold and wondered if our absence might give an impression of stand-offishness in the district. After talking to Angus we decided we must go.

Eleanor baked a cake, we all had hot baths and got the big sleigh with the old team up to the house. The sleigh had a large platform without sides. We hoisted Timmy's pram aboard and also a large packing case for all to sit on. We wrapped everyone up in blankets. The sleigh whooshed softly through the snow in bright moonlight. It looked like fairyland with the evergreens standing out sharply on the hill tops and the team trotting friskily, throwing a spray of snow over us. They were snorty and eager. As we neared the school we could hear the bells of other sleighs approaching from the west and south and our interest heightened as we tried to guess who it might be. Harold tied up the team while we lifted the pram to the ground and took a peek at Timmy. He was sound asleep. So we wheeled him over by a window and left him outside in the moonlight.

The school was crowded with friends from near and far. The orchestra consisted of a father and son. The boy, about fourteen, played the accordion while the father beat what looked like an Indian war drum and wore bells on his feet to add a tinkly touch. Everyone was dressed and scrubbed and shining. Children were racing around the school room madly in and out of the dancers. The music wasn't suited for modern dancing but it was an inspiration for the Spanish waltz, heel and toe polka, schottishche and the square dances. Eleanor had not been in town for more than two months and I was so accustomed to seeing her in blue jeans I marvelled at how lovely she looked in a proper dress. In fact, she was the belle of the ball. I couldn't do the local dances but I asked Bob and Eb Burles if they would whirl her around and they taught her the whole series from square dances to polkas. Dane and I sat on a bench admiring our 'bootiful mummy'. Everyone asked where Timmy was, and soon there was a procession of neighbours going outside to have a look at him asleep in the moonlight. With his pink cheeks he looked like an angel, and judging by the remarks that were passed to us from people who had gone out to visit him the wee scamp must have been holding court.

As Dane got over his shyness he joined the other children in their excited games, and they simply played until they dropped in their tracks. Then they were wrapped up in overcoats and tucked away on a school desk or bench. The ladies provided sandwiches, cake and coffee for which the men paid fifty cents. The children who remained awake filled their tummies with cake and milk. It was a grand party for the whole family. There was no need of stimulants for jaded spirits. There was a refreshing absence of formality and an abundance of good manners. Eleanor had been feeling low all week with a touch of 'flu and was just on the mend. The party seemed to do us all more good than a week-end in town.

On the way home we were singing like a bunch of school kids and the horses were fighting for their bits to get home as quickly as possible. I remembered my own youth with one or two sleigh rides laid on in the city, just for the

133

children, with a chaperone or two, and most of the ride along the city streets. How artificial it seemed now! Our boys could have this kind of a party any time they wanted. And we could always make it a family affair. I thought of these highlights and also the children's bath by the hot kitchen stove, the smell of fresh bread baking in the oven, the games they played outside on the fringe of the grown-up jobs, the pets they had, the machinery to play on, the buildings to climb and hide in. Dane and Timmy could always have this to look back upon. And as long as we were capable they would always have this to return to, some anchor in a changing world.

And soon it would be Christmas.

Chapter Eleven

EARLY in December we began thinking of Christmas. Eleanor made cakes, puddings and mince meat. We had a turkey fattening. Eleanor wanted desperately for our first Christmas to be perfect, an occasion we could always look back upon. And she was determined to establish the right touch which could develop into a custom for the family. To humour her, and because it was right, we made a ceremony of everything. We did not have to buy a tree, we had them right on the place. And Eleanor didn't want us as an afterthought to turn around and cut down any tree. The whole family must turn out to pick the right one and we must make an occasion of it.

That meant the team and large sleigh. She bundled the children up and we all started out with axe and saw. We drove up into the hills and along through the woods. On the west slopes the wind had bent the trees and we had to look farther afield for the right kind. With cries of "Timber!" and youthful play the unanimous choice was cut down. We also gathered green boughs to decorate the house and returned in triumph for a tea party. We set the tree up in our empty living room. Although the children did not

135

realize it the tree was pathetically bare. Eleanor could find only one strand of tinsel but she rolled up bits of coloured paper into balls and also hung up some of Timmy's toys and rattles. Dane also stuck branches in the snow outside, tying fat and peanuts on the tiny limbs to make Christmas trees for the birds. The boys were well satisfied, which was the main thing.

A few days later Augie Sauer telephoned from Medicine Hat. He had been working for three weeks trying to pick up some cattle for us and would be shipping in a few days. He wanted to know if our trails were good enough from the railway shipping point. We assured him they were and that we would be ready for the drive.

Eleanor and the boys had not been to town for three months, so I ran them in with the jeep. They had a lovely time in Pincher Creek looking at the toys and decorations in the stores. Dane was thrilled with an electric train. Opening our mail during lunch we found a letter from the silent partners. They warned us they had shipped two parcels which we were to open before Christmas as the packages inside were labelled with instructions. We hurried through our shopping and dashed to Cowley, worried about getting the parcels from the railway station. It was five p.m. and the station usually closed at 4.30. As luck would have it a freight train was in and the station office open. I staggered to the jeep with two enormous boxes which we had difficulty squeezing into the vehicle. We tried a short-cut, hoping to get home more quickly, and high-centred the jeep on a hard-packed snow drift, which lost us about forty-five minutes.

Home at last Harold announced that Augie had telephoned again to warn us he had shipped two carloads of steers which would reach Cowley next morning. It was too much excitement. Eleanor kept me up late that evening opening the boxes and sorting out parcels. The ones for Christmas had to be hidden, the rest opened now as the letter directed. Eleanor became a little girl again when she found all the proper things for decorating a tree, especially since she had that very day looked so longingly at the decorations on sale in town. There was enough to transform the whole house. In addition to large parcels for the tree there were many intriguing small things wrapped up for little boys' stockings. Other items included maple syrup, candied peel, nuts and fruit, such extravagant things which we had not even thought about for this Christmas. For Eleanor, striving for perfection, the picture was now complete. And she was deeply touched by the care and thought that had been put into the parcels. We went to bed in a very excited frame of mind. And tomorrow there would be more adventure. Augie's cattle were arriving.

The whole outfit was up before five o'clock. Harold caught the saddle horse while I milked, fed chickens and turkeys, watered the calves and turned them out to their pasture for the day. We telephoned Dingreville to see if Marcel could ride with Harold. After breakfast Harold took off about 6.30. I loaded the jeep with oat bundles and arrived in Cowley about 7.30. When I checked with the station the agent advised me the cattle would arrive on the way freight about two o'clock that afternoon. It was a difficult job hanging around, just waiting.

I called Eleanor and found she was having a wonderful time. Dane was helping her strip the tree and they were decorating it all over again. She told me that Dane thought the little glass balls were too precious to handle and was just skipping around the tree directing her where to hang them. I warned that the cattle would be late and I would telephone again after they left to give her time to organize a hot meal which I would pick up for the riders.

At last the train arrived and as the first carload moved down the chutes I noticed Harold for the first time get really excited. There were forty-one steers, twenty-four two-year-olds and seventeen yearlings. We didn't know yet whether they were to be boarders at so much a head per month or if it was a share-profit deal. That they were coming on the ranch and would boost the total stock to one hundred and seventeen head was the important thing. The ranch was beginning to look like a business. These steers could add to our income, improve our chances of keeping the cow herd intact next year. We might be able to meet our debts from Augie's cattle and the calves. No wonder Harold was excited.

After unloading we fed them the oat bundles and let the critters rest in the yards for a couple of hours. They had spent a long time in the stock cars and were 'gaunted up'. We talked about heavy gains in weight when we could roll the feed into them.

Harold and Marcel started them on the drive around five o'clock. They were going to take it easy as the steers would likely try to graze on the way and would stop to water at the river. I drove home and picked up a box of hot food that Eleanor had prepared. The cattle had moved well at the beginning and when I found them had covered some five miles. The boys, who were cold and hungry, welcomed their meal and a smoke in the jeep. The toughest part of the trip proved to be the last few miles because some of the animals wanted to bed down. But they arrived about midnight at the ranch where I had another meal ready for the lads.

We branded them next day and after turning them out with the calves in the smaller pasture for a spell we soon settled them down on the winter grass with the main herd. We had taken a firm step forward. It was with great satisfaction that I could write to Hutch and Arthur, the Wizard, Beaumont telling them of these developments, for back in July they had only taken my word that we would find this sort of break. I also wrote to Augie reporting their safe arrival, enclosing a demand note for $600 on the calves he had given us.

Christmas was upon us before we knew it. We had been making trips to town by saddle horse, returning with parcels and mail stuffed in sacks hanging from the saddle. The mail seemed to have more value, somehow, coming twelve miles from the post office by saddle horse. Everyone remembered us. There were letters and parcels from England, California, Ottawa, Australia, Kenya—and from all our friends in the West. "What lucky little boys!" said Eleanor, as she tucked parcels into hiding places. "You would think their parents were wealthy. Do you think it will spoil them? We must ration them out and make them last until the New Year or their birthdays. If there are duplicate toys it would be fun to take some around to the neighbours."

I can remember a later Christmas when the cattle broke into a hay stack on Christmas Eve, holding up festivities until noon next day, but this first one was indeed perfect. We had the boys bathed and in bed early but their excitement was boundless. They had to hang their stockings and set out a lunch of peanut butter sandwiches and a glass of milk for Santa. We promised that their hero, Bill Lagarde, would be up in the morning to help them open parcels if they settled down quickly to sleep. Edgar Burke had sent us a bottle of sherry, so we sat quietly drinking a toast and listening to carols on the radio until Dane and Timmy had surrendered to the arms of Morpheus. As Harold had gone out to a party we were alone in setting the stage.

Eleanor sneaked into their bedroom and came out with the stockings which we filled with the tiny parcels, sorted in two piles. We blew up balloons and hung them, with extra decorations which Eleanor had been saving, around the bedroom so there would be surprises to greet them as soon as they awoke. From all the secret hiding places we brought forth the many interesting parcels and placed them under the tree. It was midnight before we got to bed. And as we fell asleep we murmured to each other how precious was the scene in the nursery, so gaily festooned, the boys asleep in their innocence with the fat red stockings tied to their beds.

We were awake first, listening for them to stir. Then we heard them talking. It was still dark and they had not noticed anything. We could hardly bear the strain. It seemed like half an hour before Dane made the first discovery. "Timmy, Timmy!" he shrieked. "Look!" Then an excited squeal. "Mummy! Daddy! Santa's been here!"

We rushed in to watch Dane open his stocking and to help Timmy with his. It was fun for us as well because we didn't know what was in the stockings. Eleanor had breakfast ready in no time. Dane took note of the fact Santa had finished the lunch they had left. The boys seemed to think that was all there was to Christmas and were quite content until Dane chanced to go into the living room, and came running to tell us that: "Santa's been in the living room too!"

It was only right they should open a few parcels but we kept the main ones until Bill arrived. When Dane, after watching the electric train in the store and talking of nothing else since, found he had a real wind-up train and tracks, you can imagine what he thought of Santa Claus. Bill took him outside where they found the sleigh tracks Saint Nick had left in the snow.

Eleanor and I had discussed the modern thinking that tended to shield a child from the fantasy of believing in Santa but now we weren't sure. If there wasn't a Santa Claus somewhere, then there must be a fairy godmother. Didn't we feel it ourselves? As long as we didn't lie to the boys or impose on them our own conception we were quite convinced it was normal at their age to create an image out of their own lively imagination. The first time they wanted to doubt their ideas they could do so and we would help explain. We don't pretend to know all the answers and we had no evidence to refute all the circumstances with cold logic. How about the parcels under the tree? Most of them had printed labels for the boys—from Santa. What if we knew they came via express or the mail? Wasn't the evidence enough to confirm a little boy's opinion?

141

We didn't have our dinner until about three that afternoon. The telephone rang continually as neighbours called each other up on the party line to exchange greetings. Bill and the boys played with all the toys and games and read all the books we allowed them to open. The train aroused shrieks of delight. First they had it running on the tracks. Then they ran the engine alone across the floor pulling all sorts of crazy loads. Then Bill amused the family by tying a big red balloon to the engine and turning it loose. I really cannot say who had the most fun.

We have been fortunate in having four Christmases on the ranch since then and they have all kept to the high standard Eleanor set in the first. Bill has never missed joining us and each year the tree bears more parcels with his name—from Santa. Many friends have been up to visit and to meet Bill until he has become part of the family. As we have progressed our own pleasures have become more material. On a later Christmas the boys received a toboggan and spent part of the day sliding. After they had been tucked into bed Christmas night and all was peaceful Bill, Eleanor and I sat around reviewing the day and drinking hot rum punch. About ten o'clock Bill thought he had better get home. We all went to the door and gazed upon a night of pure magic. Fresh white snow reflecting a full moon from a sky that was almost blue, without a trace of wind, sparked us to mild lunacy. It was so bright out you could read a newspaper. The Rockies in the distance were etched in bold relief. "Bill," Eleanor said, "you can't go home now. We must try out the toboggan." And the first thing I knew we were climbing the hill to the rocks behind the house. Of course they put me in front and we raced down the hill at terrific speed, right to the fence of the horse pasture. I had snow down my neck, in my mouth and ears and up my sleeves to the elbow. They thought it was funny, so we had to roll around and wrestle until they were equally submerged. Then we had distance and speed competitions, singly and in pairs, and every other type of childish fun we could think up. When the toboggan hit a bump all the occupants would go flying and sliding on their own.

We waved Bill down the road about 1.30 in the morning, soaking wet and helpless with laughter as he whooped it up so that he must have startled half the coyotes in our part of the hills.

Christmas in the Porcupines is not a one day affair. We had to travel by sleigh to Dingreville's for an enormous dinner and games with half a dozen families present. We repeated the performance at Bougerolles. The hospitality amazed us. It was indeed a fine community. Christmas to us seemed to have lost the commercialized and formal modernization that editorial writers decry so often. We found people who were clinging to everything good that had been proven to them from the past, and which they recognized and accepted as such.

The Mowats had wanted us for Christmas day but understood our fierce determination to spend it on the ranch. Mrs. Mowat thought Eleanor would be lonesome so far from home. The following week, however, we went directly over the hills by sleigh and team, Harold riding the saddle horse so he could nip back and do chores. We enjoyed a splendid dinner, then played cards and had some good talk before bed. Next morning Mrs. Mowat thoughtfully gave Eleanor a treat which she had not enjoyed in years—breakfast in bed. We returned home that afternoon very much refreshed.

It is easy to slip into a nostalgic mood over the old days and use it as an excuse to cover up lack of progress. I don't want to give the impression that we prefer it that way or that living in the country as we have done has any special merits or appeal as a 'way of life'. To anyone who reads this dreamily as an escape and toys with the idea of going back to the land I recommend a recent book of Louis Bromfield entitled 'Out of the Earth'. We have learned that stock raising and farming is a cold-blooded, calculated science and no one can practice it today without good basic training and intensive study. It may be entertaining to read our account of the happy landing at Squaw Butte but it is well to remember that this ranch was evaluated by very capable men. And we have tried to farm it and rotate our pastures on the latest principles. We have also taken steps for modernization of machinery and improved blood lines for the cattle.

But had we walked in to a set-up with the latest machinery, been able to live in a modern home with all the furniture we required, the latest gadgets and services, I don't believe we would have had half the fun out of the venture. And I believe that when we do get these things after the minor sacrifices we have made we are going to appreciate them just that much more. If you agree with this reasoning it follows that we have a good balance of values, have been able to live closer to the earth with our primitive methods in this modern age.

From Eleanor's point of view, the home, she used to admire the inside of modern country dwellings and wonder

144

if we would ever aspire to all the labour-saving devices and comfort that is possible. But now she isn't too sure she wants it all. We started with a pump in the garden, hauling pails of water to the house. We filled tubs for washing, had to stand pails in the kitchen overnight to prevent them from freezing in winter. The coal dust from the stove settling on the water made it decidedly unpleasant. Whenever any visitor talked about what we were missing we could not imagine lights, running water, inside bathroom and everything laid on. After a few years Eleanor felt she could be content with just a small pump in the pantry. She had a gasoline engine washing machine as have nearly all our neighbours. The fact that I put the pump in and piped the water from the well satisfied us both. It wasn't a running water system but it was a big achievement in our eyes, and for the rest we would rather make our improvements in the machinery and stock line that would pay us dividends. A large modern home on a ranch doesn't add one cent to the earning capacity of the place. In fact, it may handicap the re-sale value. Joe Gilchrist used to say time and again: "When you look at a ranch for sale don't spend your time on the house, seeing how comfortable you can be. Look at the business side—the grass, soil, shelter for the cattle and the carrying capacity. If that is good you can work it to provide the home later. Some of the best ranches may have only a shack on them." Having said this I would like to put down the following bit of whimsy.

Bill, Eleanor and I were sitting around the kitchen "swopping lies", as Bill puts it, and drinking coffee during a lull in the winter. It was fun imagining what we could do modernizing the house if we had the means. I drew their attention to an advertisement in the magazine *Canadian Cattlemen* showing a map of Alberta with lines on it indicating the spread of rural electrification throughout the Province. The average small rancher, long used to making his own way, is likely to view the skeleton of lines approaching his district with mixed feelings as to how it will affect his present way of life.

"Some people just never get smart," said Bill. "I guess guys like ourselves always will be kind of old-fashioned. You folks are new to the Porcupine Hills and it will take time to learn that us hill-billies are different to most folks. This is a next-year country and we just don't cotton on to progress and all these new-fangled inventions other people try."

I thought about it again that evening when I turned on the radio for the news and caught another accusing blast of propaganda on the air. More Progress. This time it was a large plumbing firm in the big city advertising a choice of bathroom fixtures in a wide range of colours. Later when the house was quiet I sat back to think of the contrast between our old-fashioned pump in front of the house and the streamlined world that was passing us by. I pictured the House of Parliament at the back, built by a specialist of the Chick Sale school. Edgar Burke had described it as the only privy in the world with a million dollar view. Of course we were horribly out of date, but did it shorten our expectancy of life or cause us any real discomfort?

Then I thought of bath night. It takes a bit of planning around here. But sometimes one just gets in the mood for a bath. The winter has been kind for a spell and I have just finished the evening chores, toning up my muscles by

146

cutting into a stack of feed for the calves. All the critters are doing well and I'm feeling fit and at peace with myself. Catching a glimpse of lamplight from the house as I walk up from the corrals and sensing the good meal waiting in the cheerful kitchen heighten my sense of general well-being.

Balancing pails of milk and chop for the pigs, I reach the back shed intact. Soon I can relax. The cheerful hum of the cream separator announces my return. The boys rush out with a welcome and Eleanor appears with a dish for milk.

"How about a bath tonight, Mummy?"

"A splendid idea. But keep your overshoes on. We'll need more wood, coal and water."

I kick the snow and shovel around the drift for the wood pile and cut up some kindling. In the shed at the back I fill a bucket with stove coal and a grease pail with lumps to keep the fires in at night. Do I turn a tap for water? I do not. A pump perhaps? There is one at the well but the darn thing freezes up, the casing cracks and it always needs priming. So in hill-billy fashion I lower a bucket down the well tied to an old lariat, filling cream cans, canning pots and pails. After hauling water, wood and coal, I locate the tub in the dark shed and everything is lined up for the ritual.

In Porcupine Hills we are really up to date. We have a bath tub—not the round wash tub that was our initiation and despair, the kind that slopped water over the edges whenever we tried a new position, the cramped, frustrating little tub that caused you to wash in sections and continually try to invent new procedures and positions so that you didn't have one part of your body in hot water while the rest chilled in the icy air. No, we have a full length bath tub. Almost full length, that is, four feet long and thirteen inches deep. It cost us about 5 dollars plus freight. It was such a change after the wash tub we were convinced it was just as good as anything in the city. We hardly noticed it was galvanized iron instead of white porcelain enamel. When we spotted it in the catalogue it was immediately ordered for Christmas and the family took on a new standing in the community.

You know what a country telephone line is like, the party line that irresistibly draws one during a winter lull to listen in to an exchange of news and views. Sometimes when the rings aren't clear several receivers are lifted from hooks just to make sure for what party the call is intended. The station agent started us on the road to fame by calling up to announce the arrival of our bath tub. I can imagine and, mind you, I am only imagining, that someone's wife put down the receiver that day, turned to her husband reproachfully and said: "Those new people have ordered a bath tub. They must have put in running water." And quite likely the husband replied: "Sure, they always had it—running through the roof! Ha! Ha!" However, word got around that we had acquired a bath tub, and when we started home with it on the sleigh we met Angus by his gate eyeing us curiously.

"What on earth have you got there?"

"A genuine bath tub, Angus, and it cost only a few dollars more than a wash tub. I guess this is the first time they have been advertised since the war."

"Keep on going, friend. Don't let my wife see it or she will want one." So I went giddy-yap up the trail.

But the station agent was soon handling a procession of similar articles. (Note to mail order houses: All you have to do is spot one such item in each district. As long as the wives hear about it—and they will—you have got yourself some business.) We had to chuckle when we noticed them at our station waiting to be picked up.

Mind you, not all these tubs came into the district as a blessing to clear the way for progress. George Mowat, having to follow suit grudgingly, laid the blame squarely on the first customer.

"See here, old chap," he said, "I've been forty years and better in these hills and no big troubles—just dry years, poor calf crops and weak markets—until you came along. We always managed to make a living and we could wash out of a bucket, the horse trough, an old gas drum or the creek. Now we have to get a proper tub. Do you know how much water that takes? Dammit man, you are plumb ruining our way of life."

Later on some of them were put to better use. I noticed one outside a house in the spring full of rain water caught from the roof. And on very hot summer days ours makes an excellent bathing pool for the boys to play in out on the lawn. And it did take too much water for every bath!

For bath night we clear a space in front of the large kitchen stove. A blanket is spread on the floor, the tub is brought in to warm up, a large bath towel is hung by the stove and steaming pots of water are kept waiting their cue. Soap, brush and face cloth are set out on the blanket and all doors leading into the kitchen are closed against draughts

The tub is filled and the last act before the ritual of ablution is to open the oven door. A blast of hot air pours over the scene of operations. The stage is set.

How good it is to soak the frame after a day of riding and forking hay. The combination of soapy water, steam and hot air from the oven makes one realize the endless preparations are well spent. What a smooth dividend of well-being for such a small premium of healthy activity! Could spirit and body be more in harmony if one had all the benefits of the city cousin? Or would one have to exchange his daily round of fresh air and exercise for a desk job to achieve them?

I thought of the children having their nightly baths on the kitchen table, an assembly line procedure when they play and clown for us and we notice the development of their sturdy little bodies. I thought of the articles on water conservation, the cities that suffer a shortage of our most precious and fast dwindling commodity. Our bath water isn't chucked out the door when we are finished. More often it is saved for washing floors and other purposes. When you watch the seasons come and go and work the land you become conscious of water tables and their importance.

Maybe civilization will march right up into the hills someday, but a fellow has to look at all sides of the question. We realized how old-fashioned we were one time when we went to the city and took a hotel room. We thought it would be fun to introduce the boys to a proper bath. But when we started running the water at full throttle through the taps Timmy was terrified at the noise and wouldn't go near the monster.

So I said to Eleanor: "There's nothing like a bath on the ranch. Could you imagine everything up to date with lights and running water?"

"I could," she replied, "but it wouldn't suit the character of the house. We would have to add a room or take valuable space we are using now. I could actually be satisfied with a pump in the pantry until we enter old age. After all, to modernize completely you would have to consider how many cows in the herd would be working full time just to keep it going."

"Never figured it that way. Trouble is we read too much and that radio keeps butting into our affairs. But I know what we can do to improve things and make the work easier for you. We can compromise like the politicians. I'll buy a new lariat for the old bucket at the well."

And with that she fired a pillow at my head.

Chapter Twelve

DURING January we received a letter from Augie Sauer giving the weights, prices and shipping charges of the big steers. He suggested we keep track of the feed we used and feed them oats as well as hay to ready them for an early market at the beginning of summer, even if we had to buy the oats. After all these charges were deducted we were to split the profit fifty-fifty. Nothing could have given us a better start for the New Year than this news. Without putting up any cash or speculating dangerously we stood to make half the profit on two carloads of cattle. If the price dropped we would only be out our work and the cash value of the feed—most of it the hay we worked so hard to put up the previous summer. With the normal gains in weight, two hundred to two hundred and fifty pounds an animal, the price would have to drop very far indeed before Augie would lose his investment. The news gave us a tremendous lift. Just think if the price should go up! We fell to work with a will.

Some of our best hay was stacked on top of a hill with no way of getting it out except by a steep climb and descent. Normally we could wait and feed cattle up there. But we were concentrating on the steers. We had them cut out separately in the horse pasture, with their own salt and water, and Harold made them long feed troughs where they ate their daily ration of oats. We bought more grain at the elevator in town, hauling it out by sleigh. And with the steady old team we had inherited with the place we began to make a trail through the deep snow to the good stacks of hay. The steers were getting feed from stacks closer to the corrals but we intended to feed them every: thing we had and this meant moving down the hill-top stacks. Obviously the team could not take the slope straight up and down, so whenever we could spare the time we made practice runs, angling up to our objective, packing the trail well and judging from the sidling as well as the tipping tendency of the sleigh what amount of hay we could reasonably put on for each trip. When Harold decided the trail was right we tried our first load, using chains wrapped around the sleigh runners as brakes. Dane came along to help. During the descent, while Harold did the driving, we hung over the top side as you would sailing a dinghy in a stiff breeze, Dane putting all of his thirty-five pounds into the effort. We roped on the loads and it took ten trips to bring down one stack. Curiously enough we did not upset on the steepest part of the descent. But we did tip just about every trip, on the level when the runners on one side hit a hard drift.

Winter is the best time to break horses. We had started with the old team, Prince and Brownie, that Mr. Rhodes threw in with the deal. And when we had finally bought the place we purchased three other work horses at $50 apiece. They were 'rough broke', which meant that in addition to having been halter broke they had had the harness on. They might have had more than that but it was safer to assume the minimum. In winter one can harness a green team to a sleigh and start driving them with the least amount of noise and annoyance to the horses. The pull isn't too hard and then they can gradually be worked with loads so that they become reasonably safe for normal farm work. And they should be well broken in by the time they are hooked up to a mower.

Speaking of horses, a ranch as a matter of sound policy should always keep one or two teams around for emergency. During the winter with Joe at the Deer Creek he impressed this point upon us. In the worst winter storms you cannot depend upon power machinery to start in forty below and get through the tough spots the way a good team can. While we were struggling to keep the cattle supplied with feed in the height of a protracted blizzard the radio was giving details of one of the worst storms to hit the cow country in Montana. Later we picked up stories that sheep and cattle men were breaking out to the towns to get help for their animals dying in drifts. Some of them were supposed to be offering half their herds to anyone who could save them. Some of them just stayed in town and gave up. Cattlemen have been known to go out among their herds with rifles and shoot them rather than see them die slowly. In this case ploughs were trying to break trails through, only to have the snow drift in behind them worse than ever. Aircraft were employed to airlift bales of feed. "Trouble is," said Joe, "they modernized completely down there. No horses left. I'll bet good teams could save a lot of those herds." I think he was right.

154

My first spring drive into the mountains was lightened by amusing tales of horses and horsemen. One old timer had me laughing so hard I nearly fell off my horse. "I'll never forget when I worked on a big outfit in the North Fork," he said. "A neighbour's string of cayuses used to wander into our ranch until we got fed up driving them back. One day I told the boys I'd fix them and we ran 'em into the corral and put 'em through the chutes. We got some wire and made a good job of fixin' tin cans to their tails. With every horse loaded down with cans that sure made a noise. We opened all the gates and turned 'em loose. Mister, that was the wildest bunch of bang-tails you ever saw. They disappeared in a cloud of dust down the road headed for their home range. It was too bad for 'Barb-wire' Johnnie that he was comin' out from town with supplies on a wagon and was on the bridge when they hit it. He must have figgered it was the end of the world. I think he dived for the railings and hung on the outside. There were horses and harness and wagon all mixed up and supplies flying every direction.

"But I'll never tin-can horses again. You can laugh about it now but I sure hated to tell a lie when the boss tried to find out if we had done it. It was the only time I lied to him. The owner was plenty mad. It wasn't funny later when he sold one of the teams. A guy bought 'em and they were guaranteed plumb gentle. They were, too. Anyone could drive them on a wagon or sleigh. But the new owner, he hitched them up to a brand new mower. When he put her in gear and the thing started to click-click and rattle they remembered the tin-canning two years before. And, boy, they scattered that mower all over the prairie. I guess the pieces are still lying out on the range. No, sir, I won't ever tin-can a horse again. Somebody might have got killed. But they never bothered us no more."

Harold felt we should start breaking a second team so that as soon as the frost was out of the ground they would be ready for the sulky plough in breaking the sod-bound hay land. The plough would require four horses and they had to be hardened up for it.

Brownie and Prince, the old team, had been together so long you could not leave one in the barn and take out the other without having trouble. You also had to turn them out to pasture together and most of the time they walked along in the same position they were driven, Brownie on the left. Prince had an aggressive way about him and he was always mean to every other horse on the ranch except his mate Brownie.

We gave the green horses their first lesson in the corral, tying them up outside, which was safer, before putting on and taking off harness. The next lesson was driving. We planned to make it easier by harnessing one green horse with a veteran. We had just returned with the sleigh from hauling feed and as Harold turned it ready for the next trip he thought we might try out one of the new mares, called Babe, with Prince. We harnessed Babe in the corral again, then hooked her up with Prince. Brownie was very indignant. Then Harold drove his mixed team around the corral, turning and backing, starting and stopping until he was satisfied. He called me to open the gate and gently we hooked them up to the sleigh. Prince was strong enough to hold Babe from running away but we didn't want to spook the green horse by carelessness or break any of our old harness.

Now if we had tried to tie Brownie up in the barn there might have been trouble. I figured the best thing to do would be to tie him in the hay yard where he could watch Prince practising with Babe. The green horse was nervous and trembling but I threw open the gate from the horse pasture and Harold started them off quietly. I slipped on the sleigh as it passed and we were delighted to notice that Babe was keen, a good worker, and that she settled down quickly. We were in sight of Brownie all the time, but as Harold let them out and headed up the valley we could hear Brownie nickering and then whinnying violently. As I turned to watch him he was pulling at his halter rope, head and ears well up, trying to stand on tip-toe to keep Prince in sight. Harold decided not to give Babe too much the first day and we soon returned, well satisfied.

While doing evening chores we wondered about Babe. When the weather is fine we usually turn the old team out in the pasture by the dam and feed them there. Since we wanted to keep Babe working as well we decided to let her out with the team. As soon as she stepped out of the barn Brownie took after her. It was unusual to see him turn mean—Prince, yes, but not Brownie. This time he was the aggressor and he chased poor Babe up and down, biting her neck. Prince joined in the attack. Babe lost her head and ran into a fence. She went down and Prince stood right over her. While Harold and I watched, hoping they would get over it and settle down without injury, Babe got to her feet, slipped clear and headed for the other side of the pasture with the team in hot pursuit. Coming to the fence

157

she cleared it with a nice jump and kept on running in blind panic. With looks of smug satisfaction the old team turned their backs on her and walked sedately over to queue up for the evening meal. Later when we returned the mare to work we had to keep her with the steers. I had observed jealousy in people when a stranger comes between friends but had never seen an instance like this in the horse world.

During a spell of good weather Mrs. Mowat telephoned Eleanor about the quilting bee. It was well on in the winter and Eleanor had not been out much since Christmas. In town she used to do anything to get out of a hen party. But now she really did want to see a few women for a change and moreover she wanted to learn how to quilt. So when she asked us if she could ride over safely we assured her there would be nothing to it.

We were so pleased she could get away to this party we had the mare saddled up and tied to the hitching post at the house by dinner time. I offered to do the dishes, so Eleanor set off right after the meal on the trusty old mare. We watched her climb our big hill and disappear. When she returned about four o'clock we all greeted her, eager for details of the nice time she had enjoyed.

"Home never looked so good," she said. "I managed to ride about half a mile, but when the trail got so steep the mare was gasping for breath I got off to walk and I never did get on again. We ran into such deep snow I had to pick the way for her. We made Cabin Hill at last and half way down I was up to my waist in snow and the mare was up to her shoulders. It got worse and worse. We plunged and heaved until the poor old girl became exhausted and refused to go any further. I was really worried as I knew

158

there were deep ditches on either side of the road and the hill was still plenty long. But I spied a gate in the fence, left the mare where she was and went to see if I could get the gate open. As I tore the gate up out of the snow the mare made a gallant effort to reach me. It must have taken us half an hour to get through the gate, into the field and on to higher ground. By this time we had both had enough and decided to go home. But our troubles weren't over yet. I couldn't find another gate to get us out of the field and on to the road allowance. In the end I had to tread down the wire at the weakest part of the fence and persuade the mare to high step over it."

Eleanor went to bed before eight that evening and next day she ached all over. We felt rather guilty about letting her start out alone on such a trip without checking the trail first. It was just an incident in our first winter and almost as stupid as the time Harold took Eleanor to town in the jeep. I was baby sitting, and when Eleanor telephoned from Maufort's that she would be along soon I let Dane, four years old, go outside to meet Mummy. I thought he would wait by the gate nearest home but he kept on walking and was at our lowest gate, a mile from the house, when a blizzard and drifting snow came upon him with startling suddenness. He was just about buried by the time the jeep passed him and he would not have been noticed at all if it hadn't been for the dog who ran out in front of the jeep. We were lucky that time for it might have taken days to find him, the snow was drifting so badly. Dane was sufficiently impressed by his experience and our warnings to be most cautious after that.

In February it took two weeks of work, including Sundays, to move all our hay in close to the buildings. Having listened to tales of disaster in the past we thought it wise to prepare for the worst. We expected some bad blizzards before spring and believed that we might be caught un-prepared with inaccessible stacks of hay beyond our reach and weakening cattle around the buildings. So in addition to the ones on the hill-top we moved stacks from a mile north and a mile south of the house through steep coulees that would most certainly fill with drifting snow. By February 17 it was a mighty nice feeling to see all the feed in place for any emergency and everything squared away for the next storm. We estimated there was enough hay to last another thirty-five days at our present rate of feeding.

We couldn't keep our thoughts away from spring. In addition to the daily round we spent many hours sawing wood by hand, hauling logs from old cabins we had pulled down and filling the wood shed so that we should have a back-log when spring work started. Eleanor spent two enjoy-able evenings culling the seed catalogues and making out the order for her garden. She was anxious to try growing tomatoes, celery, green peppers and egg plant. For the flower garden she ordered Iceland poppies. By March 11 she had a feeling that spring was only a few days away. In the light of our experience since then, which has seen us battle through unusually long and severe winters, it is easy to laugh at our mistakes. But they were not stupid mistakes, just over-anxious and eager ones. Could you guess how she predicted that spring was close? The weekly washing usually took three or four days to dry. Out on the line it would promptly freeze and it was a matter of thawing out the frozen garments little by little until they were dry enough to iron. When for the first time she had a washing that she managed to dry and iron on the same day Eleanor decided it was time to start planting the seeds indoors. Harold caught the bug as well and started checking over the sulky plough. In the fall, pulling it with the jeep in the garden, we had hit a rock and Harold was worried that we had bent the frog and beam. We got the forge going in the blacksmith shop and after much heating and hammering got it fairly straight. To make certain, however, Harold took it down to Bill's place where they worked on it again.

Toward the end of March we began looking for signs of green grass. Everything seemed to be working to plan. The cows were heavy in calf and the steers looked fine. We began to pray for good calving weather to avoid losses. Cows are deceiving. They look fat, but when they have dropped their calves you notice with alarm that they are emaciated, thin and bony. I had just read an observation of this common mistake and looked at them again and again for signs of weakness. Some days when they would walk by to water with the icicles jingling on their hides we were thankful that the loyal Harold was with us. Calving was going to be a tricky business.

Just when we were feeling calm and confident on this point a fog rolled up the valley to swallow the outline of hills, fences and buildings. The temperature dropped sharply and a nasty south-east wind whipped up, bringing a blizzard. We glanced anew at the stocks of feed and studied the calendar to estimate the days of winter left. We remembered the tales of old timers recounting disasters in the past and began to wonder if we were going to pull the animals through.

Early in April, with Eleanor's seeds sprouting in the house, the neighbours began telephoning to ask if we had any feed left and if the calves had started to arrive. We had been cutting down on the daily ration of hay and moving the cattle out to find grass to supplement the difference. We realized it was a poor year for early calves when we heard that one neighbour had lost ten, another four and several one or two each.

It was dark when I started evening chores on April 9. Harold had gone riding to look over the herd and returned about nine o'clock carrying our first calf! He had packed it more than a mile, up a steep hill and down the other side, sliding and falling, with the mother in hot and worried pursuit. What a thrill it was to see the little bundle of life bedded down on some clean straw, dry and warm! We made an elaborate tally sheet beside the calendar in the kitchen and proudly marked up the first calf. You work hard all year for this one crop and after eleven months of planning and slogging away for the one objective, calves, you feel that you have a right to expect some help from the weather. Every time a calf is lost or a cow fails to produce you sadly write off a year of work and struggle for one of your units. For the cow is the basic unit on a ranch like this, and when you haven't got too many of them the loss of one calf seems immense.

It was natural, the first year, to fuss over the herd and try to do too much. Had we, with more experience, left

162

the old range cows alone to find their own hide-outs and shelter spots and not tried to improve on nature, we might have had more success. Since those days we have known cows to drop their calves in forty below, during a blizzard, and somehow manage to dry and warm their offspring and save them. Only hard, realistic experience will bring a man to the point when he knows just when to interfere for the good of both cow and calf and when to leave them alone. This account is not set down to reveal how we operate today or how one should handle stock, but actually how in our innocence we managed to do the job. It was tricky weather and we tried to do the best we could.

Next day four calves were born in quick succession. I found the second one lying in a pool of water between two trees. With the sack I always carried on the saddle I dried it off and after packing it a while threw it over the neck of the horse and rode for home. The cow followed for a way, but when the calf and I both got on the horse she must have lost the scent and returned to the trees.

The horse was very patient with that calf over his withers, kicking at him. Sliding and slithering in snow and mud we made our way down the slope. From the hen house Eleanor and Dane saw us coming and there was great excitement at the sight of the second calf. Eleanor opened the gate, we put the little animal in the dry shed we had prepared and I started off to look for the mother. But she had disappeared.

I continued riding until I found four cows together, one of which looked like the mother. But after chasing her to the corrals and bringing out the calf, she turned up her nose.

163

I began to panic that I never would find the mother. I tried three others without success. I felt that I had stirred the cow up so that she would never claim her calf and the little one would die. Just as I was getting desperate, on the last try of the day, the cow I had chosen pricked up her ears and hurried toward the calf. He gave a little bleat and there was no doubt this time the way she licked its face and remained contentedly beside him. As I came in for the noon meal at three o'clock that afternoon I began to wonder for the first time if we were interfering too much with nature.

One of our turkey hens was missing at this stage. Although we feared coyotes there were no signs of them around. We hoped she was nesting somewhere but we could not find her. The cows who were showing signs of calving in the next few hours we moved into the horse pasture for the night where we could check them first thing in the morning. Although there wasn't any natural shelter they could use the sides of the sheds to break the wind if a storm came up, and we could move them into the corral, a place we later realized as the worst possible spot for a good range cow. In the morning it was cloudy and threatening snow. One of our cows in the horse pasture had dropped her calf and it was lying in a wet spot, dead. I began to accuse myself, for the cow might well have chosen a better place out in the hills among the trees. Breakfast was a gloomy affair that day.

But just after breakfast when I was looking the matrons over again and turning them out to graze another cow began to have a calf. I shouted for Eleanor, ran to the barn for a lariat. I was convinced the beast was having trouble, and we fussed around the milling herd trying to keep her back while I was wondering how we could get her shut up or at least rope her and snub her up somewhere. Our fussing got all the animals stirred up. I wondered why in blazes the cow in question would not lie down. Then, right before our eyes, we saw the miracle of birth and forgot the poor little dead calf in trying to help the latest arrival. We dried it off with a sack and moved it to a dry bed, the mother coming along quietly.

The first calf, born April 9, was getting thinner each day and weaker on its legs. It could barely keep up with the mother. Eleanor and I got them into a small shed and closed the door. We put a loop on a hind leg of the cow and stretched it so she could not kick. We managed to get a large halter on its head and snubbed that up. Then I tried milking her—and she became wilder. One of the teats would not work until I had pulled off the scab. When we had the milk flowing Eleanor brought the calf up and we got him started on his breakfast. It was a relief to see the little fellow tie into a meal, switching his tail with delight, to see the thin little sides swell out and the cow quiet down. It was another victory, but with a heavy heart I went out to skin the dead calf. Determined not to call it a total loss Eleanor intended to tan the hide with a recipe of her own, half Indian and half *Winnipeg Free Press*. She had the weirdest collection of chemicals and nostrums which, combined with much elbow grease, she hoped would turn the trick.

The weather was decidedly unfair for our first calving, but had it been too easy we might have become careless in the following years. The unusual conditions probably afforded us a concentration of experience we might not have acquired otherwise in such a short time. It kept us thinking of other calves being born out in the hills and the need for constant supervision and fast action. Never since have we hoped so hard for a break in the weather. We were told that at this time the previous year the grass was green, that with the proper conditions it could green up in a few days.

We tried to hang on, save ourselves from losses and keep the cattle from slipping back. Augie's steers simply had to keep their weight, but for an early turn off to market we had to have green grass now. The most despairing sight was to stand helplessly by and watch the cattle constantly on the move, marching back and forth, up and down the hills, past the house several times a day, searching for another blade of green grass. They would get a small taste of it, eagerly search for more, and then go on the march in single file again, milling around to tear up any tiny shoots that were discovered. Their system seemed to demand grass. They had no taste for hay now. It was grass they wanted—green grass. And the weather was standing still. It wasn't winter and it wasn't spring. If it would only do something. . . .

Suddenly the weather changed, but not the way we wanted. One of those storms that all ranchers fear, an April blizzard, descended upon us. The cows that have calved are weakened, they are losing their winter coats and the rest are trying to make milk. Then you face a blizzard that with a diabolical twist of fate discourages all your good efforts and intentions. It was our worst storm of the winter and the snow piled right up to our windows. No forecast came of

166

its clearing. It was like kicking a man after knocking him down. The only bright spot for us was that no more calves were expected for a week or more and that those we had were flourishing. When the storm finally cleared I found the turkey's nest out in a stack. The eggs were cold, and as there was no sign of the hen I figured she must have been blown clean out of the country to perish in the storm. I brought the cold eggs up to Eleanor. It was just another blow to test our patience.

We were still digging our way out of the mess when the hen strutted by. Where she came from we never did find out. But she was hopping mad and indignant because she couldn't find her eggs. Eleanor hoped she wouldn't be too discouraged to try again.

And that seemed to point up a maxim for us. We must keep trying and set ourselves an example. We couldn't let a little thing like our first winter get us down. In the long wait through the deadly hours of twilight before spring the months of blizzards and cold behind us had faded into insignificance.

Chapter Thirteen

THE CHINOOK

With beef on the hoof at thirty cents,
It's the best they've ever been.
But, damn it all, if this cold spell lasts,
I'll be broke 'fore the grass is green.

The cattle stand with a hump in their back,
Each rump to the stormy blast.
Their backs are shingled with frozen snow
And my feed pile's near its last.

Don't seem to me those critters have
A hell of a lot of sense.
They'll drift on the range, then stand and freeze
In the corner of some fence.

Or they'll bawl all night around the shack,
'Till they drive me near insane.
Then, come daylight, I load the rack
And feed them all again.

I don't want to make a trip to town
'Cause it's thirty-two below.
But I'm getting short on T&P plug
And the grub pile's mighty low.

I ain't no hand to be saying prayers,
But I think an awful lot—
God, bring along an old Chinook
With a wind that's good and hot!

It must have been my banker prayed—
He's been worried about my loan—
For today there's an arch in the western sky
And the wind has begun to moan.

The mercury's fifty-five above
And the snow is beginning to go—
Yipee! I've seen the winter through!
Let the good old west wind blow!

—*A. L. Freebairn,*
Pincher Creek.

OVERNIGHT, it seemed, spring started busting out all over.
With the most startling, dramatic suddenness the warm
chinook wind came pouring over the mountains from the
south-west, licking up the snow with a greedy tongue. The
world of white disappeared. The warm wind unlocked the
earth from its long sleep; we could feel it stir and come alive
sluggishly. Heat waves shimmered, and higher up brought
the melted snow from the steep coulees in clear, merry little
streams that joined together in a mad, headlong dash for the
valley below. Our dams filled right up, the first time the
large one in front of the house had held so much water,
and the overflow rushed wildly through the lower pastures.

The rapid thaw created havoc for some good people
farther down. Claude Hammond had a shed and some
buildings washed away but managed to move his garage to
higher ground when it threatened to go down Tennessee

Creek. Our ducks, who had been so bored all winter, lost no time getting into the large dam and amused us with their antics. They refused to come in at night and all hands were employed keeping an eye on them to find out where they were laying.

Eleanor began a collection of turkey and duck eggs to set under broody hens. She kept them warm in boxes under the kitchen stove, turning them every evening. And she was 'proper mad' that our hens would not turn broody and nest on the eggs. When Gus Dingreville had brought up his income tax forms for me to type he had presented us with a couple of broody hens they could spare, but after the trip over our rough road one of them had been shaken out of her broodiness. Eleanor could have used six more.

The space behind the kitchen stove and under the oven became an important scene of operations on the ranch. At various times it has sheltered new-born calves, who were chilled through and had to be fed a raw egg and stimulant, through a frosty night under its benevolent warmth. It has harboured the weak peepings of baby chicks and ducklings just breaking out of their shells, boxes of little puppies and kittens. It was a corner that attracted the boys like a magnet. They would lie on their stomachs for long spells, gazing with wonder at the new world of hope and struggle.

The house was deserted during the day. Eleanor could only retreat to the kitchen for the meals. She built a cold-frame outside our bedroom window to which the garden plants she had started in the house during March could be transferred. Harold and I donated a whole day to Eleanor, raking the lawns and yard by the house, removing the ash pile, the tin cans and accumulated debris. We hauled fresh earth to bank around the woodshed and the garage and flat rocks for paths while Eleanor tore up the hop vines in front of the house. In their place she planted her Iceland poppies, sweet peas and lilac bushes. And all the time we worked for her we were restless to hook up horses to the plough and begin breaking land.

As soon as we could break away from Eleanor's type of spring fever, on the excuse that we had to plough up her garden first, Harold and I got busy with the sulky. We oiled and greased it, rigged the hitches and tightened bolts. Then with a brick and coal oil we scrubbed rust off the share until it was smooth and shiny. A clean share is easier for the horses, it doesn't pick up dirt and it turns the sod over clean. Harold was still worried that it might not plough straight, in which case we would have to take it to a black-smith in town.

At last we were ready, and he decided to try it with Prince and Brownie alone on a small piece of land in front of the house. When the team was hitched up Dane and I raced ahead to fetch Eleanor from her garden. Harold turned on to his line and settled himself in the seat, called to the team and threw the levers so that the share dropped into the soil, cutting its way to proper depth like a warm knife in butter. Eleanor and I danced with joy while Dane dashed along in the furrow behind, very much excited. Tippy the collie raced around almost under the horses' feet as they pulled evenly, heads down, breaking the first furrow. We were all pleasantly intoxicated by the feeling of spring. We knew that no one else in the district would consider working on the land so early in the season, but we had a large job ahead, breaking some twenty-five acres of old hay land in a rich

171

bottom. If we were going to take off a crop of oats by fall we had to start now. The others had tractors and large modern machinery and they only had to work summer fallow. We had land to break.

When Harold made the turn and started back towards us he was wearing a big grin. The museum piece that had cost us $2.50 worked perfectly. It was a fine feeling to be starting spring work on our own land. He then ploughed around the trees by the house and turned up the patch for Eleanor's garden while I took the young team, hitched them to the stone boat and began cleaning out corrals and feed racks. Right after the noon meal we intended moving down to the big field to start ploughing with the four horses. The twenty-five acre field is half a mile long and we expected it to take about three weeks to plough and disc. With interruptions from the weather and other sources we could not say just when it would be seeded, but as long as the horses could stand up to the work we hoped to spell each other off at the job.

When the weather clouded up at noon we turned to the radio for a forecast. Rain or hail or snow could be expected! See what I mean? We had to forget ploughing and move our last remaining stack of hay into the horse and cow barns to keep it from spoiling, as the top had been taken off. In the middle of the afternoon George Mowat arrived, riding over Cabin Hill with his son and daughter. Mrs. Mowat had to remain at home to run the brooder stove for a hundred and fifty day-old baby chicks. We discussed our plans for the year. George told us of the close calls some neighbours had experienced, getting down to their last fork-full of hay before the weather moderated. We laughed at some of the

172

weather forecasts we had received. Admittedly it is difficult to call the weather accurately in this neck of the woods, but George was amused when I repeated one cautious broadcast that announced: "Cloudy, otherwise clear." "By Jove, I could handle that job myself," said George.

Next morning a thin blanket of white lay on the ground. But it was warm and we spent the morning in the blacksmith shop, sorting trays of bolts, checking the post drill and wrenches for any emergency break-down. After the noon meal we hitched Prince and Brownie to the sulky. Harold started down the road while I followed with the green team. It is quite a trick to hitch four horses abreast to pull the plough. Watching Harold I wondered if I would ever get on to the complicated system and if the time would ever come when I could do all the jobs myself. There seemed no end to the business of learning and the multitude of trades to master. It made me think of the costly mistakes I should most certainly have made without Harold's help during the first year and reminded me that his presence was the best insurance we could buy.

The question came up of how to place the two teams to the best advantage, as Babe or Gertie, the green horses, might cause the old team to wander from their straight line and make a crooked furrow. Unless the start was right, with a half mile to go, the ploughing could end up in a horrible mess. And how long should one work the horses for the first week until they had hardened up? I had not thought of that.

I expected Harold to make a round, down and back, and then check his horses. But he started easily as if he had all the time in the world. Half way down the field he stopped to look at his furrow, check the horses for harness and hitches, before proceeding to the bottom. After making the turn he stopped again and sat down to roll a smoke. He didn't seem to be in a hurry at all. On his return he seemed quite pleased with the team. He gave them a ten minute rest. They had done a mile, but the two furrows made such an insignificant mark in the large field that I began to revise my estimate of the time the job would take and wonder if we could really get it seeded for this year.

"Were they hard to handle, Harold?"

"Babe tried to wander, but she'll get over it. And that Gertie isn't pulling her weight. I might have to change her around with Brownie."

"It seemed to take so long. Do you think we can finish the job in time?"

"Sure, if we keep at it. I'll have to poke along like this for about a week until they get hardened to it. We'll have to keep graining them and we might be able to borrow another four horses, but we wouldn't have enough grain for them all. No, I think we can tough it out with these horses unless one of them gets sick. I'll keep on until dark and give them lots of rest."

"Okay, fella. I'll go riding and check on the calves and I'll be out later with some sandwiches and coffee."

This business of calving was a much safer proposition now. They all had an even chance. One only had to ride around, and if a cow looked suspicious it was smart to pass just close enough to look at her bag for signs or check a new calf to see it had sucked. If these signs were normal you could tally another. The exception is the odd heifer having trouble with her first calf.

I saddled the young horse and started out. The older calves were in a group, lying on the warm ground in a perfect pastoral setting or racing in circles kicking, bucking and bunting at imaginary butterflies. Now here is something a townsman finds hard to believe. The cows with older calves join up together on the range. Coyotes are always lurking on the fringe of a herd, and although I know of no authenticated cases where they have killed a new-born calf there has always been enough suspicion to leave the question one for controversy. Certainly they clean up the calving grounds and will feed on a dead calf, and I have known one case where they worried a heifer who was down having trouble with her first calf and another where they ate a still-born calf right near the mother, who was helpless. Some cowmen call the coyote a nuisance and a danger. Others like them around to keep nature in balance and clean up carcasses.

If you want to see range cows on the fight at this stage, just take a dog out amongst them or walk alone on foot. The cows, as I say, join up with their calves, but they also have to spend many hours out grazing to keep up the flow of milk. Obviously the calves are safer in a bunch and the cows cannot all leave together. So they arrange matters just like any well organized society. They leave a couple of baby sitters. Joe had told us about this but we thought he was pulling our legs. When the opportunity arrived to observe this in our own herd I spent many hours trying to figure it out. Each day a different pair of cows were with the calves. Did they run a duty roster? How did they know which cows were on duty for a particular day? Had they some means of communication? I never could find out. However, it is done. They manage to change the jobs regularly and each day I would find a different pair of mothers lying in the midst of the calves, chewing their cuds, while most often there wasn't another cow in sight. Most would be grazing, some would be away over at the water, others would be taking salt. What discipline made the calves remain behind with the baby sitters? Why didn't one lonely calf walk away looking for its mother? We have often discussed this question without coming up with a convincing answer. And don't think for a minute that you can get away with anything. The old girls know and trust the rider who appears daily amongst them. But try to dismount anywhere near and they will be on their feet. Approach one of the calves and the peaceful scene changes abruptly. I have tried it alone and also with the collie dog. The moment the old cows on guard smell trouble they let out a bawl. The calves get to their feet and group around the baby sitters. Over the hill the rest of the mothers appear like magic, on the run, and with short little soft moos they call their own calves, pair off and disappear out of sight. If you follow one the cow will put her head down and paw the ground. That should be warning enough. The wild ones aren't even scared of a horse. City folks generally show more respect for a bull out on pasture but he is a sissy compared to a good matron with her calf.

With or without calves the range cattle usually keep together. A cow or young heifer will only go off by herself to drop a calf. This day I noticed one alone and tried to ride by at an angle without showing too much curiosity. Out of the corner of my eye I could see a calf had been sucking. I expected to see that or the cow 'making bag'.

Now I wanted a look at the calf. As I rode up into the trees the old girl was watching me unobtrusively. She was a cunning one. I hid in the evergreens, changed position before peeking out at her and noticed her start around the side of the hill on a trail. She was either going to check on her calf or lead me away from it. I moved along the hill top to keep her in sight and was perched on a rim-rock when she spotted me. I backed the horse up. When we looked again she was nowhere in sight. We moved along the edge but there was no trace of her, and as she had been quite a bit below us on open ground it seemed as though she had just vanished in a few seconds. I stayed on top but moved back to a point where I could see the place we had picked her up. It was uncanny, the way she had given us the slip. As we turned I did a double-take as we nearly bumped into her, standing by a tree right on top beside us. She must have moved quickly to get there, and after staring at us defiantly she pretended to be interested only in grazing. I tried to move her or get her excited but she would not let on. She had us buffaloed, and she knew it.

When I finally found the calf, about fifty yards away and well hidden, I decided to show the cow who was boss by moving them into the bull pasture for observation. It was a big heifer calf and lay doggo as a baby elk who has this same instinct to lie rigid when danger is about.

I lifted it to its feet and it showed plenty of life. The trouble was to steer it. Of course I should have left it alone but I started it down the hill. It kept veering back to its bed and the old cow began to act belligerent. After chasing each other on and off the hill several times I finally worked them to the flat west of the house where Eleanor saw the struggle and came out to help. The cow saw her, charged full speed, with head down. My good wife looked like the bear cub that tried to run in several directions. There wasn't a tree or fence to climb and I had to put the horse into high gear to get between the cow and Eleanor. The horse just managed to turn the old girl and I had to escort my wife back to the house, both of us scared, while cow and calf trotted back to the trees. It had been my fault entirely. But we were learning.

We didn't lose any more of our own calves, though probably it wasn't my fault we saved them. But we had one more loss. Angus had come up with another deal for us. He wanted Harold to give him a hand for a couple of weeks digging a well to get water on his summer grass. He offered us a shorthorn heifer, which we could use for a milk cow, and her calf. In this case we collected the wages long before doing the job and moved them up home. As the calf had been born recently we started right in to break the heifer for milking. We tried to play the game of 'range dominoes', as Mr. Bennett had described it in his book, by matching up the shorthorn calf with the range cow whose calf had died. But the cow would not have anything to do with the stranger although we spent many hours tying up the cow, keeping her alone in the barn with the calf, roping a hind leg and dragging up the calf to start the meal. Sometimes the game works and they settle down together so you can turn them out on the range to their mutual advantage. But this girl was stubborn and continued to fight. The calf was willing but only made headway so long as we were there to supervise and hold them together. Perhaps there was too much supervision. We tried every trick in the book, including the old dodge of dressing the new calf in the hide of the one that had died, hoping the mother would accept it on scent. But it didn't work. The calf had been kicked so much it gave up trying altogether. We had to switch it to a 'pail bunter', raising it on skim milk.

One day the bull came along and opened the barn door. The calf bolted, found its real mother and filled his little tummy to bursting with rich milk. It was a terribly bloated sick little animal that night and Harold worked late trying to save it. When we went to bed that night he thought it had a chance, but it was dead in the morning. So Eleanor had two little hides to tan.

All this time the grass was greening up at a terrific pace, the buds were coming out in the trees, among the cattle you could hear the tearing sound as they ripped up the tender shoots. The grain farmers lamented the late season but everyone conceded it was a perfect year for grass and hay crops. Harold kept on with the ploughing, up and down, rest ten minutes, up and down again. On the half mile strip the belt of rich black loam gradually widened. He did not want me to spoil his nice straight furrows, so I was allowed to make only one round at a time. I kept working at the cattle and repairing fences where the big drifts had knocked them down.

An old cow showed up with bag trouble—too much milk for her small calf—and had to be milked once a day. She was big and tough and it required time and patience to get her snubbed up. One day the rope loosened. She didn't strike me so much as lift me bodily in the air with a hind leg and when I stopped falling I landed on a very hard rock. That put me on light duties and I took the opportunity of travelling to Lethbridge with some neighbours. It was fun to see The Wizard and Hutch again. The former told me the V.L.A. were very much pleased with our progress. I walked into the Government offices without a care in the world. This time there wasn't anyone ready to shoot us down in flames. Mr. Miller had the same old smile and twinkly eyes. He wouldn't let me go as we talked and talked about the highlights of the winter. He was impressed by the number of cattle we were running but we didn't try to figure anything out. Both of us knew we had a heavy load of debts but it was impossible to estimate our probable income. There were too many factors involved for the sharpest of pencils.

One old timer had told me: "Some mighty good cattlemen with sharp pencils have figured themselves plumb out of smart deals. They worked it all out on paper that feeding steers would make money and figured it for two years ahead. At the end of the first year the prices dropped and instead of sticking with the plan out came their pencils again. They figured their losses and carried them over into the second year. Then they decided to take the loss, halving the disaster. So they sold. Next year the price went up and they had lost their shirt. But by this time they were busy on another big programme, and so help me, all the time they were in business it went like that. No, son, it doesn't pay to be too smart with the pencil. Keep on working the place and producing cattle. We are producers, not distributors or financiers or merchandisers. When cattle are ready for market sell them at the best weights. Keep your books straight, pay your bills and leave the sharp pencils to others."

Early in May Eleanor came running out in the rain to tell us some thrilling news she had picked up on the radio. The Minister of Agriculture, according to a news broadcast, had opened negotiations for the export of beef cattle to the United States. It sounded like just the break we needed. How good it would be for us we could only guess. At the best it could bring our prices up to parity with the American market. The least we could expect was for our prices to hold firm at the present level.

It was just a year since we had first laid eyes on the ranch and a fine Saturday afternoon reminded me of the fact. I asked Eleanor to come for a walk, ostensibly to look for more calves. We strolled up the valley reminiscing.

"Do you remember when we first drove up here and thought it was too big a place for our resources?"

"Yes, and you tried to turn around and drive away, you coward."

"And you, my precious fool, repeated Augie's words about buying it anyway and worrying about it after. He didn't know we had no right trying in the first place."

"Remember the letter with the cheque for five thousand and the nightmare when you drove to the Hat? It all brought things to a head, Hutch and Beaumont came into the picture and so many things happened at once we didn't know if we were coming or going."

"So many things happened that summer I don't want to leave this place again, ever. The set-backs you get here you can see or estimate. You can fight them or wait them out.

181

But never again do I want to experience the uncertainty and blind horrors of the position we found ourselves in then, with no place to turn."

"Well, sonny boy, here it is. It's all ours and will become more so each year. When I leave this ranch they are going to carry me off, in a pine box."

This was light-hearted banter, but it was spring. We had never felt so sure of ourselves, so healthy, tanned and hard. We were both working harder than we had ever worked in our lives but we had never been happier. Edgar Burke had written to remind us of the struggle ahead and had added that we would always be looking for the day when we had it cleared and could turn around to buy ourselves furniture, a car, clothing or do anything we wanted with money. But he warned that we would look back on these years, when we were struggling for our ideal, as the best. He ended by hoping we would stop once in a while to realize we were having the best fun right now.

Turning back toward the house, walking arm in arm and marvelling in the beauty of the place and the wonder, which will remain always, of the peace it has brought us, we stopped on a rise above the house. The picture spread before us was framed by green slopes angling from east and west. The dam, smooth as glass, reflected green slopes and blue sky. Below the dam the freshly ploughed field took on a new aspect. Eleanor swears the soil had a purple tinge to it. It looked so clean and neat. On the slope above it the willow and Saskatoon bushes reminded us of heather and the flat field on top had young brome grass growing thickly. On the other slope across the valley from the ploughed land we swept our eyes over the horse pasture and fixed on a pair of black and white statues. They hardly moved, and we knew that Prince and Brownie were trying to get in the act by completing as pretty a picture as anyone could wish. In the middle distance to the south the strip farms were changing colours as the machines varied the pattern and in the far distance the foothills rolled up to the turrets of the Rockies. Very clearly we could make out the Gap leading to Waterton Lakes National Park and at the end of the mountain chain, way down in Montana, Big Chief stood proudly by himself, looking like a bluff and hearty friend.

Eleanor broke the silence. "Oh, but I wish I could paint and had the time to drop everything and just stay here for a couple of hours to capture all that colour and beauty."

But our life seemed to swing sharply from the sublime to the ridiculous. Eleanor and I had a yen to try some fruit trees. Shortly after our lovely walk with its touching moments I used the plan as an excuse to satisfy a hidden frustration. I was going to plough land on my own. I was going to show Eleanor what a man she had married and prepare new ground for the fruit trees. We had an old walking plough that would need only Prince and Brownie, Harold was away for the day, so without telling anyone I hitched up the team and hauled the plough into the garden. After making one horrible pass at it, when the plough insisted on twisting and turning, popping out of the ground and digging in too deeply, I called for the good wife and asked her to handle the lines. She tried to drive the team while I wrestled with that infernal implement. I couldn't get on to the hang of the thing and as my temper mounted it became obvious the blame should be put on Eleanor for faulty driving. Any husband knows the trick. It is one of the cardinal rules in marriage for supporting the male ego.

The more we tried the more I criticized and the wilder the plough snaked around, in and out. I threw off my shirt to fight it, and Eleanor left in disgust to continue putting in potatoes. I tied the lines together, put them over my head and really settled down to fight. I was plain mad by this time and the steady old team settled down to following the best furrow. At the end of each row I collapsed on the grass, fighting for breath. It was like wrestling some two hundred pound giant. But I stayed with it until the strip was black and had to do the chores very late in the dark. Eleanor and I weren't speaking so light-heartedly that evening; in fact we hardly said a word, and next day I was stiff and sore. Imagine anyone in his right mind wanting to be a farmer!

Harold had been in town trying to get the jeep fixed, and when I showed him the plough next morning he said it didn't have a breaker bottom and could not turn the sod over properly. He ran over the ground with the sulky repairing my mistakes.

I had figured the only way to learn was by starting with the walking plough to get all the angles, then riding the sulky on a post-graduate course. Each year I did some work with the walking plough and finally caught on to it, but the initiation could have been a lot easier had I known about some minor adjustments. Bill came up once and caught me practising, dropped a bar about four holes and after that the share didn't dig in too deeply. From then on it was easy to control. But from that time, whenever I begin to act big and talk like a successful rancher, Eleanor interrupts with: "Don't forget your experience with the walking plough." Perhaps that is why most ranchers seldom lose their modesty and humble bearing. The business is full of walking ploughs.

We had the land ready for seeding by the first week in June but heavy rains delayed the final job. When Harold finished ploughing I did the discing in a couple of days with the same horses, and then he dragged the field with large planks. Rain continued to plague us until the middle of June but we were fortunate in not being so dependent upon the weather as grain farmers. We wanted this field for feed, and green feed would suit our purpose as well as threshed grain.

We had come full cycle on the ranch. From now on everything we did had a precedent. The jobs were looking familiar and our big interest was in improving the procedures and mastering the trades.

Chapter Fourteen

ELEANOR's poultry business started to pick up. In the garden beside the house she had a regular nursery with special little houses for the baby fowl and this gave us all a chance to study their living and eating habits. There were twenty-four chicks, ten ducklings and nine turkey poults. Of all these the ducklings proved the most interesting and amusing. Ungainly as they are on land at first, they are forever chasing butterflies and insects through the grass. We raised them all in the garden, fearing that down by the barn they might be wiped out by coyotes and chicken hawks.

In those days we had quite a few peculiar ideas about animals. For instance we believed that ducklings should not be allowed near water in the early stages of their growth. Where we picked that one up I cannot say, but the family was horrified when I scooped up a few of the little ones and dumped them into the rain barrel for an experiment. Even though they swam around happily Eleanor was not entirely convinced, conceding them only a pan of water to play in. However, as in most cases, the animals themselves soon taught us the truth. After many weeks of care with the

186

first hatch we stood speechless when a mother duck took her day-old brood waddling in a solemn, ludicrous procession towards the dam where they entered the water and proceeded to cruise in line astern. Another queer idea was laughed into oblivion.

When an early hatch began to arrive Eleanor brought them up to the kitchen, to the great delight of Tim and Dane. One particular egg seemed to be a dud, but when I suggested throwing it out Eleanor was indignant. It fascinated her and she kept close watch. When more than a reasonable time had gone by she gently made a tiny crack in the shell. There was a slight struggle inside, so she peeled off a piece. More struggle, and more help from the budding scientist supported by an interested audience of little boys. And weren't they proud when the little spark of life teetered uncertainly on the palm of her hand and they all rushed out to show me the triumph! Eleanor named it 'Little Albert', kept it warm in the house and fed it pablum for a few days. She took a lot of teasing for wasting her time. "He will never make much of a duck, I know," she said. "He is much smaller than the rest to start with and he doesn't grow so quickly, but he is well worth his feed in entertainment. Take a few minutes to watch his antics. He is just like a Walt Disney character."

During the early part of the summer that was his role exactly—falling into buckets and holes, tripping over a blade of grass, trailing behind the flock, always getting lost but always trying valiantly to keep up with the rest, stumbling at high speed and skidding along the ground on his beak in his frantic efforts. Little Albert was pure clown. After watching him day after day running into disaster, losing his mates because his little legs would not go fast enough, Eleanor said: "Now there's one duck I shall never be able to eat." But the ducklings graduated to the water and other interests crowded them out of our minds except for an occasional count. Keeping track of all the additions to our family was like trying to take in all the acts in a three ring circus. By late fall Albert was just another duck; in fact, we could no longer positively identify him.

Spring made us think also of visitors. There had been no time for such amenities last summer, although we had been able to show a little hospitality to a few friends. Hutch had been out on a flying visit one Sunday to inspect the layout, the Wizard of Oz had shared the doubtful comforts of the crowded cabin in an attempt to straighten out our problems, and the good priest, who had put heart into me during the lowest ebb of our fortunes, had come out for a few days to help with the haying as he had promised. Eddie and Edna Goodfellow, who had given us such a big boost at Manyberries, dropped in late in the fall to see how we were making out. We had just moved into the house and were ashamed of our inadequately furnished home. Now that we were getting settled it would be fun having old friends inspect the place.

We hadn't long to wait. Before the roads had dried two cars came churning up through the mud bearing the faithful Harry Hargrave, two men from the Livestock Insect Laboratory in Lethbridge and a business man from Calgary. We decided to start a guest book. It was a great joy to be able to let off steam telling Harry about our experiences. They were all amused at the trial and error methods we had adopted during calving, at the machinery we had obtained, and while Eleanor produced a memorable meal we had a lot of laughs.

Dick Painter capped our stories with an account of his setter bitch having pups. It started by his asking if we needed any dogs and his assurance that he could fill our order for any number up to fourteen. I bit into that one for more details when I noticed the twinkle in Harry's eyes. Then Dick launched into his story. The setter had been readied for her maternity in the basement of Dick's house and when D-day arrived he was hanging around to offer encouragement. "I was fairly calm and controlled when the first few arrived," he related, "but then they kept coming and coming and it seemed to be going on forever. Finally I couldn't stand it any longer, rushed to the telephone and called the vet. All I could shout into the 'phone was: 'Say, how the hell do you turn this thing off?' "

During my last visit with Mr. Miller in Lethbridge he had asked if he could send a reporter out to take some pictures and get a story for the veterans' paper. When I talked the proposition over with Eleanor she reasoned that if there was a story here I should write it myself and try to sell the article. Perhaps it would make some mad money for us. While Harold was ploughing I sneaked into the cabin and battled it out. When it was finished we didn't know what to do with it except use it for starting the fires. Eleanor said she was sure she had read worse stuff but I didn't ask her to remember when. This reminds me that one time I asked George Mowat which farm paper he would recom-

189

mend us to take. "It depends upon how many stoves you have," said George. "If there are two fires to start you need to subscribe to a couple of them." Anyway we borrowed a stack of Mowat's magazines and after some debate we sent the article to MacLean's Magazine in Toronto. Of course they didn't buy it but the article editor was nice enough to take the trouble to write a long letter in reply. He pointed out why it would not suit them in its present form and that they might be interested if we found time to do it over on the lines he suggested. He told me not to forget there were a lot of other old squadron types around there too. He also mentioned that it might sell elsewhere, and wished us luck.

This was almost as exciting and as good for the morale as the thrilling letter from the silent partners when they sent us the big cheque. I put in some nervous hours on the typewriter and wrote the thing again. It didn't give us any big ideas, but on the strength of the encouragement we made a deal with Bill to buy his cream separator for $20. Up to this time Eleanor had been taking the cream off by letting the milk stand in cans. So with a few magic words that considerate article editor unwittingly increased the butter production of the ranch. We mailed the revision, and as we were swinging into high gear again with the farming and haying promptly forgot about it after a final sigh of relief that we had not told anyone about the incident.

Early in July I began to receive letters from an old Air Force chum living in Montreal. I had met and known well a number of fine French-Canadians in my time but Charles topped them all. We had come together in England at the repatriation depot, spending our days playing squash and swimming, our evenings trying to master the game of darts. Charles was the perfect companion. We talked about youthful canoe trips and skiing week-ends in the Laurentian Mountains of Quebec. Charles described the life he experienced in lumber camps when he was working his way through college. We tried to conceive the perfect peace-time job that would take us back to those outdoor activities. Not being aware of conditions at home we tried to turn back the clock to the life we remembered best.

We travelled home on the same ship and our friendship deepened. Charles was very modest about his war service and would not be drawn into the exuberant accounts of daring experiences when the talk got around that way among the more youthful members of our party. He wore a battle dress with no ribbons showing but I ascertained he had done a tour of operations in Africa on Wellingtons early in the war, picked up an immediate D.F.C. and then gone on to Pathfinder Mosquitoes. When the young chaps at our table gave out with their hair-raising "there I was on my back at ten thousand and no airspeed on the clock" stuff, I would turn to Charles and say: "What did you do in the last war, Daddy, or did you just fly Mosquitoes?" That would generally change the subject.

One day before Charles appeared at the table I asked the boys not to talk about flying in his presence as it embarrassed him. When they wanted to know why I explained patiently that he was being returned home for 'lack of moral fibre'. So they kept quiet and avoided him like the plague. The last night at sea I told Charles we were expected to dress for

191

dinner and got him into his best regimentals with all the ribbons. You should have seen the look on the faces of those boys.

We both wanted to keep up our connection on this side too, so as soon as Charles could get away he joined us at our cottage near Ottawa while we were awaiting discharge. He visited us once more while I was trying to become a business type. He had the idea then that we should stay together and try to get into some outdoor work, but seeing me up to my neck in the business world he had kept quiet.

Our correspondence continued. Every time we found a new excitement in the ranching venture Eleanor would say: "Charles would have loved this." We hoped he was finding life as interesting as we did. But, alas, it was not so. When we separated he started up a small factory near Montreal, putting in his savings and getting help from his father and friends. After a long, heartbreaking struggle his business headed for the rocks. He was married now, had a child, and we felt our paths would never again intersect. However, we kept writing and promising ourselves a reunion one day.

His recent letters revealed a mood of unhappiness which contrasted greatly with ours. When he wrote wistfully of the fact that we were doing the things we had planned for in England while his own business was folding up and that he wished we were closer so we could talk things over, we decided to do something. Eleanor and I both wrote Charles and his wife suggesting he try to hitch a ride out west. The fresh air and exercise would help him pick up a better view of the problem they were facing. Subconsciously we hoped that he might get the breaks as we had.

About the middle of July we received letters from them both announcing that Charles would arrive the following day. We didn't have transport at the time and were haying from five in the morning until dark. We debated whether or not to ride in the following evening with a spare horse for Charles but figured it might be a cruel experience for him right at the start.

About noon the next day Eleanor answered the telephone. The station agent said there was a parcel for her and asked her to hold the line. It was Charles and they had an excited conversation.

"I'm here at last, Eleanor. How do I get out to the ranch?"

"I'm sorry but we haven't got the jeep working. Gray is out haying, and he suggests you wait in town until he can arrange transport."

"Tell me where I can get a taxi and I'll be right up to help."

"A taxi? There isn't any such animal for miles around. You'll just have to be patient and wait."

"I'll start walking then. Just tell me which direction to take."

She had to talk him out of that. The station agent took him home for an amiable visit and in the evening the elevator agent brought him out to us. It was dusk when he arrived and we were too excited to say anything sensible. He couldn't get over the scenery, the whole countryside was more pleasant than he expected. Eleanor made us turn in early and we carried his kit over to the cabin.

We were shocked at his appearance in the morning light. He seemed to have a prison pallor, a very tired and tense look. And he had aged a bit. This wasn't the old Charles. I caught Eleanor's eye and shook my head doubtfully. But she cornered me alone and said: "Now there isn't a thing wrong with him that good hard work and big meals won't cure."

We tried to be easy with him but Charles insisted on starting right in with the haying. He milked the cows, drove the teams and always remembered to do grateful little jobs for Eleanor. And how he tucked away the meals! We began to get a warm glow inside as his colour picked up, his muscles hardened, his steps became springy and, best of all, his highly developed sense of fun and delightful humour gained the ascendancy over his troubles. He began writing enthusiastic letters back to his wife, and when he met Bill, with his homespun philosophy, Charles began to develop a hard core of conviction that his future held substance.

At the same time Dane had a visitor of his own, Michael, aged seven, who arrived to spend the summer holidays with us. His father, formerly chairman of the V.L.A. Board, had helped us over some rough spots. For a present Michael brought Dane a tame rabbit, but with a lively playmate to join him in the serious business of exploration and discovery our son had simply no time for the pet. So Eleanor had to adopt the bunny, settling him in with her growing brood of chickens, ducklings and turkeys. It was interesting to notice the reaction of the two boys. Dane woke up to the fact that many things he had taken for granted were marvellous experiences for Michael, who told me that the previous summer he had spent only two days in the country and the rest of his holidays on the hot city streets and playgrounds.

No wonder he found the ranch so thrilling. We turned them loose without direction and they never seemed to stop except for meals and bed. They kept the old mare busy in the corral, riding her whenever they could manoeuvre her alongside the corral rails to mount. They built houses in the trees, discovered caves in the hills and found so much adventure we all felt younger.

Eleanor found looking after the two lads an interesting experiment. Michael's fine manners and appreciation of the place were good for Dane. Once she decided to give them a special treat—a bonfire high up on the rocks after dark. They both had a long sleep that afternoon so they could stay up late and Eleanor spent a good part of the day getting special food ready. The boys hauled a supply of wood to the site of the bonfire and we were all briefed to get into the spirit of the party. At nightfall we helped Eleanor climb up the steep slope, packing pots of weiners, beans, gingerbread and cocoa. It wasn't much of a meal for a hay crew. The two boys grabbed a bite of everything and disappeared. The grown-ups huddled around the fire in the chilly evening breeze and tried to keep up party spirits with the smoke blowing in our eyes. And where were the kids? They had just caught sight of a new haystack started that afternoon in the corral and were having a wonderful time climbing the frame of the stacker and jumping into the sweet smelling hay. Eleanor said it taught her a lesson. Never again would she attempt to manufacture their entertainment.

Charles was growing younger every day. He fitted into the life better than anyone we had known and we envied his ability at picking up quickly and efficiently the trades that had taken us so long to master. He was a natural. He loved cowboying and could stand the long hours of heavy work. The old lumber camp muscles came into play again so that he could duplicate any feat of strength. Bill thought the world of him and gave Charles a high rating.

Eleanor and I talked it over. We couldn't offer him a job here but we could let him and his family have the cabin. If Charles stayed around to help with the work the food problem would not be a heavy burden on us. What about the V.L.A.? Could they be convinced it would be a good investment to back him? Instead of putting his grant into land, perhaps they would let him spend it all on cattle. This ranch was so very much understocked another small herd wouldn't be noticed and we could run them together. After a few successful years perhaps Charles could get the V.L.A. to stake him to a place of his own. Maybe if he stayed around on this kind of wicket he would run across some old timer wishing to sell out. Charles would be just the man to arrange a time deal. Or we might find a rancher without any children who would let him gradually take over. Having him close by would be a pleasant prospect and the few years he might spend with us before going solo would certainly be happy ones. With Charles there were never any bad days, no temperament or sulks. Eleanor loved him as I did, and I am sure he was the closest thing to an identical twin I shall ever find in this world. If we could only pull the hat trick for Charles it would be a wonderful thrill.

I talked to him about it. I told him what Eleanor and I had agreed upon. He could have the cabin. We would scrape up furniture somehow, and if he could sell himself to the V.L.A. for backing he could buy a herd as large as ours and work with us until they produced enough to start him off on a ranch of his own. His qualifications were better than mine. He had put in much more time on farms, he knew the score and in addition he had spent a year at an agricultural college before taking a university degree.

George Mowat offered to drive us to Lethbridge. We hauled out our business suits, shined our shoes, shaved and bathed, put on our best shirts and ties—and surprised ourselves and the family with our appearance. As the roads were extremely muddy we walked three miles to meet George on the Snake Trail. We arrived in Lethbridge at noon and suffered on the hot pavement.

The first thing we did was call at the bank to see Hutch. Most of the talk was about the ranch and I took a lot of kidding. Hutch wanted to know what chances there were of the place breaking even this first year and of our having any income. Although cattle prices were just fair I was optimistic that we would do well with all our marketable stuff. Hutch threw cold water on my sharp pencil work with weights and prices. Then I changed the subject to Charles, explaining why we were going to see the V.L.A., our idea of running his cattle with ours, living in the cabin and sharing food and coal. Hutch kept a poker face and asked us to let him know what developed. After we left he telephoned Beaumont and they must have had quite a talk.

We made our innocent way to the Government office. Mr. Miller had been moved and Michael's father had left the service. We talked to one of the staff. He made it short and sweet. Our plans did not take into consideration the regulations as applied to the Act. Money could only be granted for stock if the applicant had clear title to land of his own. There it was, and you couldn't get around it. The man gave Charles what he considered his best advice —go back to Quebec and forget about it. If he wanted a piece of land the chances were stacked against his being qualified. Turning to me the official said it was much tougher now than when we applied. Good applicants with plenty of experience were being turned down every day.

"But how about our case?" I asked. "Couldn't you pull another miracle for this man? He is far better qualified right now than I will ever be."

"Maybe you don't know how lucky you were," he replied. "We still figure you should never have been passed and I can tell you now it was touch and go for a long time. The only thing that got you in was the fact the records showed you had been a stock inspector in the Mounted Police."

"Come on, Charles, let's get out of here," I said shakily. Boy, I thought, wait until Eleanor hears about this. I had been a stock inspector only long enough to know which end of the animal to throw the hay at.

We walked down the street with our tails between our legs. I wasn't feeling any better than Charles whose shoulders were beginning to sag. I recognized the feeling and knew that only a quick return to the ranch could dispel the gloom. But I was thinking desperately. The chap said that Charles had to have clear title to some land. I had a section of the ranch in my own name, the V.L.A. had the rest. We were going to call on the Wizard anyway, perhaps he

198

could switch the land, giving Charles clear title to that section we owned. Then we would see what could be done with the Government rubber stamps. When I explained the gimmick Charles didn't like it. But I asked him to suspend judgment until we could find out what the lawyer thought. Eleanor and I had planned a happy ending for our friend's troubles. It had looked good to us on the ranch. But our view from these hot city streets had narrowed the outlook. Charles was in what today is called a deep freeze. I would have to do the talking.

We found the Wizard waiting for us. He didn't give me a chance to say anything. He was smiling at us both and he was very kindly.

"Now let me do the talking," he said. "Hutch telephoned me. He is worried about you two. So am I. It's time for some plain talking, and as long as I am protecting the interests of your ranch I am not going to sit by and watch you lose what you have fought so hard to get. I don't want your friend to take my remarks personally for they are not intended that way, but you, my boy, are just getting started and you have a long hard pull ahead. You started on a shoe-string and although you have been lucky you are on a sticky wicket. You have a fighting chance of making it alone and you must always remember that. Think of Eleanor and the boys. Take your friend in with you and you cut your chances in half. As long as I am your lawyer that is the only advice I can offer. And you, my friend," he added, turning to Charles, "give them this break. Get back home or into something on your own. I wish you all the luck in the world but I won't stand for any deals with the ranch."

We all shook hands and walked out in the street. Every word Beaumont uttered seemed like horse sense but I felt it was a crushing blow to our hopes. I looked at Charles. With a gallic shrug of the shoulders he said: "That was the truth. It was the way I felt all along."

Eleanor was just as disappointed. We tried to think of an alternative and kept open the offer of the cabin with the hope he could find a job somewhere managing a ranch. Charles stayed on until the end of September. We picked up the old spirit and fun. His health had so improved he didn't mind returning East to look for another field of endeavour. At least that was what he told us. But I felt we were letting him down and the place would not be the same without him. He put sparkle into the life.

Bill and others gave him harvesting work. Augie took him down to his ranch near Brooks for some quick money stooking and we managed to pay Charles for some of his time here. Just the other day when I met Augie in Lethbridge the first thing he said was: "Do you hear from Charles? How is he doing? By golly, you know the boys down there still talk about him. They sure loved that guy."

I believe his letters home continued in good spirit for he had offers of several positions. But when the time came to part we were all sad. We felt so helpless because at last we had something we could all enjoy whereas our best friend had to return to an unknown future.

Our roles were reversed during the last week. It was Charles who was cheering us up. "I'll go home and make a lot of money," he said. "And when we can do it right I'll be back. Keep your chin up, Eleanor, and look after the old man. Don't worry about me. This has done me more good than you will ever know. I'm a new man now."

And off he went. Every time we saw Bill he would ask: "Any news of Charles? Gosh, but I was sorry he had to go back. He would have done all right out here, yes sir."

Charles went back to flying, bush work for an airline. Then he became airport manager but kept his hand in on the flying at the same time. They have a home and three children now and they sound happy. I hope he is making money but Charles knows that money isn't everything. We have stopped pretending that a miracle will see him out here again to settle down, but we still talk about another reunion. If we ever go East it will be for the prime purpose of seeing him again. In any generation and in any country they don't make 'em better than our friend Charles.

Chapter Fifteen

WHEN the Community Auction Sales started up for the
summer we didn't have the time to follow the trend. These
sales, held at Lundbreck, Pincher Creek and other points,
are run by the same committee and attract all the main
buyers to one focal point where the cattle are gathered. The
committee generally chooses a good loading point for rail or
truck hauling and organizes each sale so efficiently that most
of the producers prefer this type of marketing as it pro-
duces strong competitive bidding among the buyers for all
classes of cattle. You can pick them from fat butcher stock
to canners and cutters. A grower gets the same break
whether he has only one head to sell—a cow, an old bull, a
small calf—or a carload lot of even steers or heifers.

One can also sell cattle right on the ranch by having a
buyer come up, look them over and make the deal by private
treaty. Other methods are shipping them to a commission
agent in the main centres by rail or truck, consigning them
straight to a packer, or selling them to a neighbour. I
don't pretend to know the best method. We have tried them
all and they all have their points.

Toward the middle of August we had two cows ready to market. They were dry—that is, they had not produced calves—and the ranch could not afford to run boarders. As Bill was driving a bunch in to the sale at Pincher Creek on August 13 we entered our two in the same sale. It meant an early start the day before and driving the cattle some twenty miles, or less if the river could be forded. Bill knew our crowd was busy with the haying and offered to take ours in with his bunch if Charles could come along. Eleanor fixed him up with a lunch and we saw him off to the rendezvous with Bill.

Cattle must be checked in the day preceding the sale, penned for an overnight stand, weighed in the morning and sold that afternoon at the scale weight without any shrink. The buyers bid on them to relays of auctioneers using a loudspeaker device, offering so much a pound after looking them over in the ring from their stand and hearing the total weight announced. By private treaty one can try to outguess the buyer by selling at so much per head or so much per pound on the hoof, the weight being taken at the shipping scales. Generally with this method a deduction on the weight of around three per cent is made for shrink. The supposition is that the rancher toward the end of the drive to the scales will fill his animals up with water; it's a standard joke in the business. But actually the buyer must allow for shrink between the live weight at shipping point and the weight on arrival at destination, and I have yet to meet a buyer who didn't say he took a terrible beating on the shrink in any deal.

I went in to the sale wondering just what those cows would bring. This was a trial run for us. Mr. Beaumont had tried to cheer us last summer by comparing life to the Grand National. You come to a big jump—a stone wall or brush—you check the horse's stride, tighten the grip and estimate the distance to the take-off point. Then you gird your loins for the big moment, give your horse some rein and leg him over. If you have everything right and the horse is in form you clear nicely and land safely. A long stretch of smooth running lies ahead while you concentrate on the next type of jump. It is important to know the course. In our Grand National we were approaching the first obstacle, which Mr. Beaumont might have called the water jump. I thought of the genial Irishman this day and the faithful bank manager as well as the silent partners. Mr. Beaumont had written us about gathering strength for the 'lep' and I wondered if we had done all we could. Just two cows were entered, but we only had a total of thirty plus the Jersey from Dingreville and the shorthorn from Angus, none of them paid for. We had to make every jump count.

The yards were full of cattle. The buyers were sitting in an enclosed stand and I imagined they were all tough, hard-boiled characters. On two other sides were rising tiers of seats for spectators, generally filled with farmers and ranchers who may, if the price is not right, bid their cattle in and take them home again. Across from the buyers, in a small stand on the other side of the sale ring, were the auctioneers and clerks.

The sale was in progress. I found it hard to estimate the weights of the animals as they entered the ring, and as the bid kept changing found it impossible in my excitement to work out in my head the total value of the animals in question. If we didn't get a good price for ours how could I know quickly enough to bid them in? We had bought the cows with calves at foot for $125. How much did the calf weigh at the time, and how much the cow? Let's make it easier. Say the cow would be worth $100 and the calf $25. No, that wasn't enough for the calf. Then what were the cows really worth?

I wished I had remained at home like Bill. He takes his cattle in to the sale and then stays away. He doesn't even try to find out how they are selling and in due time the Association mails him a cheque. Bill always says: "If you're going to sell 'em, take 'em in to the sale and fergit it. There's no sense hanging around trying to figger against those guys."

I turned to the man sitting next to me. "How is the sale going?"

"Fine," he said. "Just fine. It's a dandy sale."

"Are you buying or selling?"

"Me? I got a little bunch entered in this sale."

"How about prices, are they good today?"

"What do you mean good? Haven't you heard the news? Hell, man, they opened the American market yesterday and there's a bunch of buyers from across the line sitting right there in the stand. The Canadian buyers are mostly keeping quiet, all but Hymie Cohen and he's sure making them pay for the cattle all right. That Cohen, he sure is a white man and he's sparking this sale."

"How good are the prices?" I asked weakly.

"Just listen to the bidding, neighbour. It's getting stronger all the time."

That beautiful water jump. I looked over toward the

205

Rockies and the friendly foothills. My, but the buyers were a fine looking crowd of men, so intelligent and kind! Everyone looked nice but I wished someone would smile to break the tension. Such poker faces—you could hardly catch them bidding. Good old Cohen.

When our two cows came into the ring I sat on my hands in case the auctioneer might think I was bidding. My nose was suddenly very itchy and I fixed my eyes on the back of one of the cows and kept them there until they bored holes in the hide. Bidding opened at twelve cents. If the cow weighed only a thousand pounds that made it $120. Don't think about it any more. Don't look at anyone. Keep your eyes on the back of that cow. Now the bid is at fourteen cents. Holy cats! as Bill would say. Why didn't I make Eleanor come in with me? Now it's sixteen cents. When are they going to stop? Seventeen now and they are tapering off—and a quarter—and fifty—seventy-five. Now it's eighteen cents—eighteen—now a quarter. It's got to stop some time. Keep your eyes on that cow. What a beautiful old girl! Gosh! they got past the quarter. It's eighteen-fifty. Sold to Swifts. I wonder which one of those fine fellows bought them.

"Two cows. Put them in pen six."

I fell off the stand and walked around behind. Should I find the buyer and shake hands with him? Pull yourself together, chum. Look at all those other guys with poker faces. These are big operators. Try to behave like a cowman. All this excitement for two lousy cows. What would Bill or Fred Hewitt think of you now? Hang on to the old cow's tail, boy, and she'll pull you through. I wonder if there's a telephone out here? Must call Eleanor—and won't Hutch be pleased! But how about the cheque? I should get a receipt or something. The animals aren't mine now.

"Pardon me, but do you go to the office or something when you sell cattle here?"

"That shack over there is the place. They hand you a slip."

"Thanks."

I waited in line for my ticket. It read: "Weight 2500—2 head—cows branded 7C—. Price per cwt. $18.50—Total $462.50." I didn't stop driving until I came to our village and telephoned Eleanor from there. I kept taking out the ticket and looking at it. Then I drove home with a present for the boys.

Before I knew it I had the sharp pencil out trying to figure out future profits. Cattle had almost doubled in price. It didn't seem likely the price would drop as quickly as it had risen. Professor Ewen had it figured for a strong three year market. I wished I could talk to him now. No one had really believed the price could jump like that in a few days. If it would just remain strong we had the problem licked. Those calves we had bought would be all profit. We didn't think of the gruelling days of plodding work now, the storms of winter and the bitterness at losing a calf in the spring. If those prices could only hold up we couldn't help but make it. The calves we bought with the original cows might pay for the whole works. They were in the mountains and would come out in October as long yearlings. And how about the fifteen head I had bought from Augie at $40 apiece? Augie's steers, too. We should try and guess the gains they had made and compare the weights and prices he had paid for them against the new market. Eleanor talked me into putting the pencil away. It was all guess work.

Augie left the steers on the ranch until the end of August. We stayed away from town and kept hitting the ball by putting up feed, building fences and riding regularly through the herd on the summer range. At the end of August the big Dane drove up to the ranch. He had telephoned Calgary and decided we should ship by rail from Cowley direct to the packers. He bought another few carloads of cattle from Bill and the Dumont brothers, so there were plenty of riders to make the twelve mile drive. Augie spent two days with us. In the air now was a different kind of excitement. He had a good look at the ranges, the type of grass, and admired the cattle. When he returned to the house he said to us: "I can tell by the look of the place and the animals that you and Eleanor love it here and are putting your heart into it."

After driving to the loading point the cattle were weighed and Augie cleared the shipment with the railway and the stock inspector. I was disappointed with the weights of our steers and Augie admitted they might have been heavier. But he added: "Don't worry about that. Weight isn't everything. It's the price that counts. We are both going to make money on this deal."

Charles rode my horse on the drive. The boys had to do a lot of cutting on foot, separating our beasts from Dumont's and Bill's. Then they had to drive half a dozen or so at a time on to the scales. Charles loved this part of the work. It is like blocking on a football field. A man has to start and stop quickly, all his reflexes must be working. After the cattle had been thoroughly worked over one of the last of the big steers to go on the scales got on the fight—really on the fight. All the boys, born and brought up with cattle, knew the signs and quickly disappeared up and over the corrals. But Charles stood innocently in front of the big animal wondering where everybody was. One false move and the critter would have charged. Finally Harold poked his head out through the gate leading to the scales and the steer charged in there. They sure laughed about it after and asked Charles if he had been a bull fighter. He thought they were all sissies, quitting the country like that.

On our return to the ranch Augie wanted to know how much hay we had fed them. I didn't want to charge the hay against the deal as without it we could both show more profit. But he insisted, marking down $600 to be paid us for the hay.

"Okay, Augie. You want to pay us $600 for the feed. I owe you $600 for those fifteen calves. Do you want to call it quits?"

He put down his pencil and looked straight at me.

"I was only kidding about those calves. They are a present. You weren't going to pay me for them anyway. I should have told you when you sent the note but I just tore it up and threw it away."

"Now look, Augie. I came to you for a business deal, not charity. You can't do that sort of thing. It isn't fair to Ethel and Pat. It isn't that we need it either. And by doing something like this you are going to stop us from coming to you for any more business. Please, Augie, think of us. You have done too much as it is."

The big fellow was obstinate and I could hardly face him. The tension of the previous summer seemed to well up inside and break again as I remembered Augie and Tip fighting to hold our dreams together. There were strangers present, talking quietly in a corner of the kitchen, and I didn't like it. I was choking back emotion and fighting the tears. There wasn't a reason on earth why he should do this.

"Now listen, Gray. And you come here too, Eleanor. While you were flying bombers over Germany helping to win the war I was home here making money with a lot of others. I felt pretty badly when I couldn't help you better last summer. Ethel and I want to do this for you and this is the first chance we've had. Use your head for a change. I'm making enough money on the big steers."

"I can't do it, Augie. It will spoil everything."

"Listen to him," he boomed. "So it will spoil everything. You mean it will make Ethel and I both feel good. What's the matter with you, man? If you can't take the calves you can't stop me making a present of them to Eleanor. The business is finished. You get $600 for the feed. I'll take out the cost of a young bull for you and mail you a statement on the steers when I get the prices from the packers. Don't try to talk about it any more. I wish I could give you a statement now but I'm kind of slow at the pencil work."

Augie and his party got in their car to drive away. Eleanor and I were so overwhelmed we just stood dumbly by the back door to wave them away, feeling helpless that we could not thank him properly. Then Davey Gibb, retired sheep herder and rancher from Medicine Hat, turned to us and in his soft Scottish accent said: "Good luck to you both and take a tip from me. I have known the big fellow a long time and we always travel together. Don't try to thank him. Mon, he's awful embarrassed right noo."

About September 11 we had a cheery letter from Augie. We had both done well on the steers. Our share was over $2,000 and for two heifers and two more dry cows we had shipped to Burns at the same time there was another $850. We sent the cheque in to Hutch at the bank and advised him we still had our yearlings in the mountains. When we brought them out the middle of October we were going to try and market the steers if the price was still high. We also had to find another deal for cattle the coming winter. We had plenty of feed. The field Harold had ploughed made a pretty sight. One of the best crops of oats in the country. If we cut and stacked it all for green feed we should be in a position to bargain with anyone. Augie had told us to write him when we knew what the picture would be but we were shy about bothering him again. If he really wanted to put cattle up here he could do it any time but, as I wrote to Hutch, it might be better for us to make our own deal with a stranger.

The North Fork Stock Association, to which we belonged, ran our cattle through the summer in the mountains behind the Livingstone Range. The Association was organized by arrangement with the Department of Lands and Mines. We had a rider up there all summer and with extra men to help he began gathering the cattle toward the middle of October. On the fifteenth the members collected at Maycroft, some twenty-five miles from the ranch, to cut out their cattle.

I rode over the hill to Mowat's place and we eased our horses around through the hills to the Walronde flats in the North Fork valley, across the large open range to the bridge, where we joined strings of riders converging on Poverty Flats, the site of the annual round-up.

It was a colourful scene with so many groups of riders on their best horses, gaily dressed, winding up the road towards Maycroft. This annual affair brought friends together who might not have met once during the summer, and on recognizing a friend a rider would rein in and wait to exchange the latest gossip. Often entire families would turn up in a dashing group—parents, sons and daughters together. Generally it is a sparkling fall day in the beginning but later it too often turns suddenly wet and cold. Chaps, spare sweaters or jackets and a ground sheet are standard equipment. As this is one of the oldest stock association round-ups in the country many cars also gathered, passing in continual procession from the towns round about. Occasionally when a larger outfit employing half a dozen riders roared by on the road in a large stock truck with saddle horses aboard, someone would say ironically: "Dudes." Spirits are high, for this gathering signals the end of the summer activity. It is always fun to watch a good horseman like Ernest Lank on his grey fire an imaginary gun at a flight of ducks overhead, then gallop madly in pursuit, swinging a lariat to rope the birds.

At Maycroft Hall the ladies of the neighbouring ranches were assembled and had a hot noon meal waiting for us. The saddle horses were turned loose to stand with drooping reins inside the hall yard. Everyone sat down to a good meal on a table running the length of the hall. From ten thirty in the morning until one in the afternoon the long line of cattle filed by on their way to the flats. At the end of the meal the association rider and officials who had been detailed to help in the count reported their tally to the president. Generally the tally is about a thousand head.

After the meal we all gathered in the yard to yarn a bit and twist smokes. Groups tightened cinches and arranged their holding points outside the main herd. The president and secretary or an appointed round-up boss decided which outfits should cut first. They usually send five men in at a time to cut for five outfits, then change after a couple of hours. At this stage I noticed two ranchers with brand new saddles. I hoped no one was paying any attention to the plug I was riding or the ancient saddle I had borrowed. As everyone crowded around to admire these fine examples of the saddle-maker's craft it was amusing to watch the faces of the two proud owners, each trying to judge the other man's saddle without being too obvious about it. They both looked like a couple of ladies in church at Easter wearing the same exclusive piece of millinery.

When we moved out for the cutting and holding of cattle I found our place and learned we were putting four outfits together. Tom Heap, the vice-president, would cut for himself, Baillie, Mowat and me. Burles and Lank were together and they had four riders. Noel Cox was by himself, with Mrs. Cox riding to hold the cut. Lynch-Staunton, the president, had the whole family out. And there was the former polo star, Harry Gunn, seventy-four years old, doing the cutting for the Elton ranch in an old pair of sheepskin chaps. He could still ride hell-for-leather and put younger men to shame. The round-up went on for hours, changing outfits, holding cattle, chasing dogies back into the main bunch. About four o'clock it began to snow and the brands became hard to read. I thought we would never get finished before dark.

When the herd had been narrowed down to a half dozen unidentified dogies and no one could see the brands, the ropers came into the picture. Sometimes the young bloods try their hand at roping the big ones, eager to test their horses. Some years you can watch a master at work such as Frank Macdonald, one time world champion cowboy, who has a ranch at Maycroft. His rope, horse and technique are thrilling to watch.

This was a different game to roping a calf in the corral. There was generally a big animal out there in the open and the horse had to be as good as the man. And in front of such expert critics the man had to be very good indeed. I was mighty glad I had left my rope at home. When the critter was strung out with ropes from two horses and thrown on its side, willing hands would pile on. Harry Gunn or someone who knows all the brands in the country would clip the hide for evidence of ownership.

With the round-up finished we trailed our herd to the Jack Baillie ranch, trying to light a smoke for comfort against the wet, the cold and the misery. I didn't know what to expect next but followed along, turning the cattle into pasture for the night, stabling the horse with the others after helping to feed and water.

Coming into the large, warm kitchen like drowned rats we were met by Jack Baillie who stood by a cupboard at

214

the other end of the room firing dry clothing at us—jeans, shirts, sweaters and socks.

"Here, boys, try these for size and get into something dry," he called. "And I suppose you would be mad as hell if I poured you a hot rum."

Sitting in the living room before a roaring fire it sure felt good to be a rancher. And from the kitchen came the aroma of good cooking. Baillie was the perfect host, with a fund of stories about the old days and witty asides for any remarks we could make. Bob Burles, the Lank boys and Tom Heap rounded out the good company that evening and none were spared Baillie's playful barbs.

What a business, this ranching! The entire trip was like a convention. We had a good evening and a fine sleep. In the morning after a bang-up breakfast we were away for the long drag home. The cattle poked along, giving a man plenty of time to think to himself or talk shop with his neighbour. He could play his horse around if he wanted to school it or just amble along. If the weather was bad you could always find shelter for the stop to eat your sandwiches, and we generally made Mowat's in time for dinner.

On this trip we were three head short on the total but until we made the cut at Mowat's we would not know whether one or both of us was short. It was too dark to cut when we arrived, so I proceeded on the last two miles over Cabin Hill for home, both horse and rider feeling stiff and sore. I could tell how my horse felt by the way his eagerness for his home pasture fought against a shorter, choppier stride. There was no doubt about my own stiffness when I had to climb off and on at the gates. Mrs. Mowat had telephoned ahead, so Eleanor had a bath ready with lots of hot water. And after a meal I collapsed in bed.

Next morning when I returned for the cattle we cut on foot from Mowat's corral and found we were short the three head. Everyone tried to cheer us up. "Don't worry," they said. "The betting is that they will show up on the second drive." One man even offered to buy the three missing head, he was so sure we would recover them. Another told us the grass had been too good in the mountains that year and a lot of the animals had worked so far back on the ranges they were difficult to round up. But still we worried about them.

George felt badly at this loss in our first year, and when he attended an auction sale at Lundbreck the following week made a point to look up the rider for the Association. The chap told him he had definitely located two head of ours and would be bringing them out soon. George rushed to a telephone and called Eleanor. We accepted the fact that we would lose one head our first year in the mountains.

Another week went by. Finally the rider had a telephone message relayed that our cattle would be coming to Poverty Flats where we could pick them up Sunday. It was an unexpected surprise to find three animals instead of two, all in good flesh, and we trucked them home jubilantly to join the others on our best grass. When the oats had been cut and stacked we turned them into the stubble to pick up loose grain and they had weeks of splendid grazing.

There were twenty steers in the lot. We wanted to keep the heifers to build up our breeding stock, but if we could sell the steers at a good price we would be over the hump our first year. We didn't know whether to ride our luck through the auction ring or sell at private treaty. Only two more sales were listed for the year. I tried to get buyers to come out and make an offer but no one showed. Perhaps they figured that we intended to invite competitive bidding, which was correct, or perhaps they wanted to delay coming out until the auction sales had finished and we would not have so many alternatives.

The truth is we did not know which way to play it. One day I was convinced it would be safer to sell them by private treaty. A few days later I thought the auction sale method would obtain the highest price, providing there was a good turnout of buyers. But here we were at the mercy of the elements because a bitter, raw day would keep them away. Some very cheap buys had been made in the past under these conditions. And this time we weren't selling a couple of head. Twenty of our own steers, representing a year of work, would be in the ring at once, and there had to be the right kind of buyers. Not all of them would be bidding for a lot of twenty. They weren't fat enough for the packer. A steer man might buy them for stockers or a feeder might see a quick turnover in them. On the other hand they might just look at them and consider the steers were carrying too much flesh for the big gain they desired.

So we argued it out at meal times, the little boys probably unconsciously picking up the business, and vacillated from day to day. When no buyers showed I decided to take a chance on the last sale of the year at Pincher Station and entered the lot.

We didn't have much time to brood over it. We had to sell them to pay Mr. Rhodes the first instalment, square

217

our running expenses, taxes, payment to the V.L.A. and all the rest of our commitments. Hutch had kindly refrained from sending us monthly statements reminding us of the mounting figures. I had only a vague idea how bad or good the picture might be.

Some of the neighbours thought we should keep the steers another year and with their gains make about $75 more a head. Even Gus Dingreville asked me if I had thought of that. I told him we had, but it was a good axiom of business to take a profit when you could and keep up with the payments. He liked the answer and said: "Now you should think like that." Then he told me about two ranchers living side by side on almost identical places. One fellow sold his beef every fall, "Never mind the price," Gus said, and paid his bills. The other fellow used to hold them over, carry a note at the bank and speculate. The former is still here, comfortable and prosperous. The other chap went broke and quit the country.

Then we received a fateful telephone call. It was Hutch. "Did you take on any more cattle?" he asked.

"Haven't had time to scout around," I replied.

"I've got a natural for you then. A new customer has been in the bank. A business man from a small town out here about forty miles. He took in some two year old steers on a debt and doesn't know what to do with them. He can't sell them right away and feed lot charges are too high. I recommended your place and you better not waste time looking him up. I told him the bank would guarantee your integrity but you have to make your own deal. What? Go ahead and ask him for all the gain. He wants to get them off his mind and you can take them for a year without putting him to any expense. Let me know how you make out."

I lost no time driving down to look at the steers. They weren't as good as Augie's bunch but they would start us out with prospects for the second year. I saw the man and made arrangements to meet him in Lethbridge. We would weigh them there, sign a contract and I would take over the shipping charges from there to the ranch. Yes, I could have all the gain. He would set down their weights and the price at which he took them over. If the selling price next year was greater he stood to make the difference at the weights when I took them. I could have all the rest. We could also brand them as ours.

Back home I barely had time to figure that one out and type a sample contract when there was a telephone call to meet the train with the shipment in Lethbridge. There were thirty-one head, averaging 890 pounds. I billed them out to our station, raced for the ranch and arrived about midnight. Of course I had to lose an hour of sleep to tell Eleanor about the excitement.

Harold and I were up before daylight doing chores. I borrowed an extra saddle horse from Angus and trotted for town. The train arrived about 10.30 that morning. After giving the cattle a short rest we started for home. It was dark when we arrived at the calf pasture and turned them loose. And tomorrow our twenty steers had to be in the yards.

Next morning we had to make the same kind of early start with the steers for Pincher Station and the last auction sale. We were galloping to the next big jump in our Grand National. It was crowding things too closely but it was exciting. I had not had time to think about the market trend or prices. I didn't know if we were doing the right thing leaving the new steers without supervision and not branded. We concentrated on the drive. By road it was twenty-one miles, but by cutting across country and fording the river we might cut off six miles of the journey. Taking them to market you don't try to make a quick trip. You let them ooze along, grazing as they go, trying to hold their weight.

When we arrived at the river after the noon stop a thin layer of ice held us up. The cattle would take to the water, cross the ford to the ice, try to climb on it, break through, then turn back on us. After having them mill around in the river and slip by the horses to return to the starting side, we gave it up. We found a shoal of gravel on a bend farther down and headed them for it. They finally made it. After a slow climb out of the river valley to the flat prairie on top we had to bear a cold east wind. The last hours of the drag were most unpleasant, and when we arrived at the sale yards stiff and cold we had to hold our bunch for an hour to take our turn. Bands of cattle were converging from all directions. Everyone seemed to have waited for the last sale.

I dreaded the thought of riding all the way home again in the dark, but fortunately Bill arrived in his truck with a load of cows and offered to haul our ponies back into the hills for the return trip. I was so grateful I didn't even try to climb into the cab, which was crowded, but rode with the horses. It was cold out there, and slippery because the cows had been painting the floor. If I had been a horse with a preference I should have chosen to leg it home.

I was in early next day for the sale. I compared our steers with others in the yards, watched the buyers arrive and talked to ranchers about prices. You can't tell how a sale is going to go. Sales on succeeding days at two points fifteen miles apart vary widely. The prices at the beginning and end of a sale often show a marked difference. One reason they tag off at the end is that no buyer wants to be left with part of a carload and they often sit back rather than risk it. Most ranchers, therefore, like to have their cattle come into the ring at the beginning. I found that ours would not be entering until near the end. A bad sign. This time I wasn't going to be caught in a whirl of excitement at the mounting bids. At the ranch we had agreed to be satisfied with twenty cents a pound. If the bidding didn't make that I would take them home. I told Hutch we would get twenty-two but he said we should be well satisfied if we got twenty.

The sale started off fine, but the afternoon wore on and I watched them bringing in cattle from pens at the other end of the yards. It looked as if they would never get around to ours. I caught one of the officials at the sale and told him I had to get a good price as it was our one big chance to get through the year ahead of the game and our steers were first class. "Why don't you get the auctioneers to announce it as a special bunch?" he said. At a recess he called them over and I talked to them. Warren Cooper and Don Ball took my name and location, saying: "Sure, we don't mind making an announcement like that when we are asked."

Then I walked in among the buyers in their special stand. Bobby Dogterom, who knew I was trying to create interest,

221

said in a loud voice: "I hear you've got some nice stuff entered today?" and winked at me.

"They sure are," I replied. "Twenty head of the best yearling steers in the sale." I wondered if it was ethical to act like this and thought of my neighbours and friends in the stands. But what the hell, we had to sell them and every cent would count. We hadn't taken all those chances last year to let it slip through our fingers now for lack of nerve.

"Hello there, Mr. Cohen, I hope you are bidding on yearling steers today."

"You got some in, Mr. Campbell? Sorry I'm not buying that class but I'll speak to Mr. Neufeld. He might be interested."

Mr. Neufeld came up to say: "Are these steers you entered out of the original Rhodes cows? I know that class of stuff and I may try to buy them. Twenty head eh? I'll think about it."

Bobby and I stood by the small door leading into the buyers' stand. We let buyers in there, but when one tried to leave before the end of the sale Bobby turned him back. "You don't want to leave yet," he said. "Those good steers haven't come in yet."

I thought they would never get around to ours. Then I could see them. Bobby was now down in front, bang in the middle of the stand. He turned to look at me and I pointed and held up two fingers. They would come in after the next lot. When the gate finally opened Bobby turned and in a loud voice called: "Are these your cattle, Gray? Boy, they sure look classy." They did indeed, and I was proud of them filling the ring. A nice even bunch.

Booming out over the loudspeaker came the voice of Don Ball. "Now, gentlemen, we have a nice carload lot of special long yearling steers from the ranch of Gray Campbell in the Porcupine Hills." Golly, I thought, they are all we have and these guys must think they are hand picked from a hundred.

"What ranch did you say?" called Bobby.

"The Campbell ranch," said Warren Cooper, while I stood there, rigid, breaking out in a cold sweat. I could hardly take a breath. What a pressure play this was, and perhaps in bad taste.

"What will you start with this classy bunch?" called Don.

And away they went, like a horse race when you have put all your money on one nag to win. They opened at twenty, and I could breathe again. The bidding went up slowly by quarters to twenty-one. Now there were only two buyers left trying for them, but they were stubborn. I dug the nails of my right hand into the palm of my left. Twenty-one and a quarter, and a half. It slowed down. Now twenty-one fifty—seventy-five. Twenty-two. It made twenty-two. And a quarter. It's going to stop there. No, it isn't—it's a half. Twenty-two and a half. Is that it? The auctioneer faltered, was about to knock it down at the half when someone must have given him a secret signal. It went to twenty-two seventy-five, and stopped there. My heart picked up the beats it had missed. Yipee! What a price! We made it.

"Sold to Mr. Neufeld for 22.75—Next lot."

Bobby walked by and gave me a pat on the back. He was in a hurry to return to Lethbridge and he was late. Cohen walked past me and gave me a big wink. Everyone seemed happy. I put my hands over my head and clasped them like a boxer towards the auctioneers. Mr. Neufeld came up and shook hands. He is a neighbour with a big ranch on our east border, and I thanked him. Someone mentioned it was the top price of the day.

There was no point in hanging around. I picked up the slip, asked Mr. Ryan to mail my cheque to the bank and crossed the railroad tracks to Cook's Trading Company store. We had been running groceries on the cuff there for months. So I asked for our bill. I added $200 to the amount owing, wrote a cheque with a flourish, told Gladys it was her turn to owe us and hoped it would carry us through until next summer. Then I went to the station and sent a wire to Hutch at the bank before racing home. I was tired from all the riding and the tension during the build-up of uncertainty. It was all over now and I was going to have a real night's sleep.

Our first full year on our own ranch was drawing to a close. We could look back and count our blessings. What a Christmas this one would be. Harold was going to be married and would be leaving us in the New Year. But we were confident enough now to carry on alone. And best of all Harold would be paid off to the satisfaction of every one. Whatever the future held our Grand National could be summed up by thinking of the next two years as the same race with the same set of jumps. We had taken them all cleanly in the first round. We faced a winter of smooth running between jumps and we had been over the course before. We knew what to expect.

There was a letter dated December 1, 1948, from Hutch in Lethbridge. Here is what he wrote:

224

"Please be advised that we have today received a cheque from Pincher Creek for the sum of $3,076.67 which we have placed to your credit. We were very pleased to get your telegram and were very proud of your effort. The only thing is don't think Santa Claus is going to come around every day in the week. I have seen some lucky guys in my day, but I think you rate the top of the list. More power to you, and let us hope that they keep coming. You had better see Rhodes and give him a cheque for your payment."

Maybe Santa doesn't come every day but in our case he was around when we needed him. Maybe it was luck and I won't deny we needed it. But if it takes that much worry and tension to have that luck I would rather trade it for a few more cows and look for excitement elsewhere.

Chapter Sixteen

IF YOU LIVE high up in the Porcupine Hills of Southern
Alberta and your wife wants to have another baby, you
think twice about the idea. In fact you think about it a
long time, considering all the angles—especially if you are
a greenhorn starting out on the cattle ranch you have always
wanted and have gone through enough anxious days and
long, sleepless nights to get it. You don't want any doubtful
incident to crop up that might throw out of balance the
delicate scales weighing the odds of success or failure.

Eleanor's arguments can be convincing, especially when
she has a long string of victories behind her. She has the
happy faculty of making everything work out the way she
wants it to. But her only argument was based on one female
proposition, viz: we have the perfect spread for bringing up
children; we are happy and busy doing the things we have
always wanted to do and it would be extremely selfish not
to share the fun with another little papoose. So goes the
argument of a woman! She did not elaborate, but the theme
of being selfish rankled. She thought the work would not
suffer too much; in fact we would hardly notice another

baby in the set-up with two active little cowboys, and she insisted there was enough love to go around.

I had to think of the economic side first. A baby would certainly set us back financially. We had sacrificed personal comfort to getting a start with stock and equipment. The roof needed shingling and the living room was still unfurnished. Plans for a set of harness for the team and for a second saddle horse would have to be shelved. How much more could I afford to disrupt our programme in order to avoid being accused of selfishness? I kept thinking over the idea while riding the hills working cattle and tried to avoid discussing the subject with my single-minded squaw.

Eleanor had not included an obvious clincher to her argument. Our home is in Alberta, a province which encourages babies by paying the hospital bill in maternity cases. That meant we wouldn't have to worry the first two weeks! Then we heard about the Health Society in Pincher Creek where the nearest hospital is located. We could join as a family for $40. That plan would see us through sickness, accidents, operations up to a certain amount for one year. The secretary, Mr. Graham, who runs a barber shop in Pincher Creek, said the society would also take care of part of the doctor's bill for a maternity case.

It began to look possible on the economic side. But the second consideration, and the most important one, was Eleanor. She said it was all nonsense about having a baby being hard on a woman and ageing her. She pointed to classic examples in the district and said she would just have to be sensible about not overworking. Besides she thought a family of five would be perfect. She wanted to have her family around her while she was still young enough to be included in their play and schemes. Dane was born during the war so she could have something permanent from a wartime marriage. Timmy was born because she wanted a playmate for Dane and was apprehensive that an only child would be spoiled. Now she thought that another one would be good for Timmy and remove him from the danger of being the youngest in the family. But where was a fellow going to draw the line?

While still at the discussion stage I saddled Pete one day and fogged down the valley to visit my good friend Gus. Gus was by way of being an expert on these matters. He had come out from France about forty years ago to work as a miner in the Blairmore district. After getting a stake in the mines, where he turned out more coal on contract than most men twice his size, he had turned his hand to farming in the Porcupines. From the start Gus had kept a fatherly eye upon our ranching venture, his sound advice and material help easing us over many a rough spot. We seemed to be his particular charges. He consistently tried to shield us from the reverses he had suffered. "Sometimes," he said, "I no got twenty-five cents on the pocket. I work hard and we eat and when I get the chance to buy some land I go to the lawyer and say, 'You fix the paper, I get the crop and pay for the land,' and the lawyer, he say: 'Gus, I fix.' "

Gus has a good spread now. If you think hard work shows on a man, you should see him now at sixty-two and watch him put in an ordinary day. In spite of his own busy season he always had time to run up here. If he noticed we were going to take ten days to get our green feed stacked with snow threatening to pin it down in the fields, he would arrive at daybreak next morning with two teams and racks and a son in tow. And we would slap the stacks up in a couple of days.

"How much is that, Gus?"

"No matter how much. You should be have the feed up, and it's done. You no pay me for that. Some day I get stuck and you help me." And so it goes. We don't keep a record except in our hearts and it makes for a happy community. You share the good and the bad. But I am glad to say that we try to keep the score balanced. The hills are full of neighbours like Gus.

He is the expert for the current problem, surrounded by children large and small, seven of them, ranging from twenty-five years to a baby of two. As I rode into the yard I noticed Gus wading through kids to feed his pigs. He waved a greeting and we went to the corral to talk. I told him that Eleanor wanted another baby but I thought it wise to wait until we had a few more years behind us.

Gus looked indignant. "You should not be worry about having kids on the farm, you know. I tell you that is easy. Maybe you milk another cow, raise a few more chickens, put some more potatoes in the garden, grow more vegetables. I tell you that. No, you don't worry about the kids. That is easy. You only worry when they grow up."

It sounded simple enough, so I had another talk with Eleanor. In the city you decide which hospital you wish to patronize and which doctor you would like, always on tap at the other end of the telephone. You have the corner drug store to supply your needs, friends to pamper you and help to be obtained. In our country you wonder if you are going to be able to get to a doctor or hospital when the chips are down, whether you can make two or three trips out before the event. You also take into account how you are going to meet the emergency if you cannot span the twenty-one miles.

The first thing to decide was when to have the baby. Eleanor's idea was to rule out spring because the gardening, chicks and ducklings are her special department and the calves' arriving would conflict with her own event. In the summer there is branding, haying and threshing with extra help around and she couldn't imagine taking time off. In the fall there are cattle drives, the movement to winter range and the activity in throwing a diamond hitch around the place before winter storms can strike. We agreed that March would be best; that would give us a fighting chance of the weather breaking and enough time to recover for spring. So we ordered a baby for March delivery, 1949 model.

Until September we were much too busy to think about the matter. We didn't even get in to see the doctor. The weeks raced along in pleasant weather and healthy activity. After the first snow we fitted two sets of chains on the jeep, filled up with anti-freeze and hauled out a 45-gallon drum of gasoline. Our main worry was the lack of a road from the ranch buildings to the Snake Trail leading to Cowley which is on the main highway. The old bridge crossing the coulee a mile below the house had been taken down before we bought the place and our councillor was trying to get equipment to put in a culvert and fill. Temporarily we were driving through a field that had been ploughed and worked to give us feed. The long stubble was sure to hold the snow. The neighbours telephoned one day to say the graders were working this way and we became quite excited when they repaired the road to our gate. But the 'cat' was somewhere else, broken down. The culvert was used on another job, and then the weather closed in with a vengeance. We realized there was no use hoping for a miracle; the coulee would not be bridged during 1948. We were now on our own in planning an avenue of escape.

After each heavy fall of snow I would rush through chores, warm up the jeep, and with shovels aboard break another trail out through the stubble. Angus, our closest neighbour a mile and a half below, would join me in the trail breaking and we began to find out just what the jeep could do under adverse conditions. At this stage we were quite confident the little vehicle would see us through unless the weather worsened. But, just in case, we talked about relays of teams for a dash by sleigh to cover the twelve miles to Cowley. I brought a team in off the range and began hardening them. The Bourdiers and Lapointes, farther down the trail, offered to stand by with fresh horses.

My sister in Ottawa was getting ready to come out here in March to look after Timmy and Dane. She planned to stay long enough to help Eleanor over the first few weeks back at the ranch. Excitement mounted as January blew itself out. The snow deepened in the hills and the drifts increased. The party line telephone was busy after every storm. Neighbours riding out to look at their cattle would check bad drift points. A few days after every blow someone would dash to Cowley for mail and supplies—by sleigh from higher up, by car or truck from lower down. Thus we got up-to-date reports on road conditions.

On January 17, after winds reported up to 80 m.p.h. had messed up the drifts that had been so nicely dug out, Angus and I bucked the trail with the jeep and shovelled the spots where we could not detour until we came to the little wooden bridge by Arthur Wright's place. Art couldn't resist the challenge of trying to get to town, so he jumped in with us and, knowing every inch of the country from this half-way point to Cowley, guided us through with only one long stop. We made it downhill in three hours and returned home in two. Then followed a couple of weeks when the weather brought temperatures varying between 34 degrees below and 20 above, more snow and more drifting.

On January 31 I managed to drive to Angus' place where he and George Mowat persuaded me to go in with them by sleigh. It was a cold trip but took the horses little more than two hours. At the beginning we joked about the diggable drifts along the way but farther down the sight was depressing. The trail was plugged solid on the straight stretches, the snow covering fence posts and reaching into the fields where there was a chance of a detour. The snow was hard, but not hard enough to carry a jeep on top, and the wind had formed wave-like crests and hollows that tipped the sleigh over on one occasion. We had to find an alternative way out quickly.

We began to make up routes. There was only one outlet, through the stubble field, but to get into the field we had to by-pass the dam, and the trail winding below the dam would fill up with snow after every wind. East, west and north are steep hills which blow clear on the west slopes but on the east lie deep under drifted snow through the winter.

By ruling out the trail to Cowley and concentrating on a straight run to Pincher Creek, twenty-one miles away, one is faced with the same problem—how to cross the coulees and how to get out of our alpine bowl around the worst drifts in order to find a coulee crossing. The greatest obstacle is the Tennessee Coulee. One road crosses it linking up with the road to Cowley and the parallel north-south road that leads to Pincher Creek. We had to try and get a way out on this road.

It doesn't take long for the neighbours to rally in an emergency. That spirit seems to be the essence of life in the hills. On February 3, Louis and family arrived by sleigh. While the children played and the women gossiped we set out with the jeep. We spent hours digging drifts and had some breathless moments riding over the top of deep spots on hard-crusted snow. By the time we were ready to eat shoe leather we reached Tennessee. It was plugged solid on the east slope and we estimated it would take a day, possibly two the way we were feeling, to dig it out. Louis suggested turning north, if I thought the jeep could climb through untracked snow, to follow the ridges higher up the coulee. By trial and error we broke a trail to Buck Baldwin's corrals. Buck had watched our progress and had managed to get in a team to come to our aid by the time we reached his camp. We found a way across the coulee by his buildings where the cattle had packed the snow, and after checking the latest report on the road returned home at 4.30 in the afternoon to demolish a good roast.

February 4 brought light snow and cold. This was to be the last visit to the doctor before the event. We were all up before daylight. Louis rode up to Angus' place and George Mowat came over the hills by team. We left Dane and Timmy with Angus' good wife, and with the extra men for emergency ran to town on the trail we had opened the previous day. The news was good. Eleanor was fit and the doctor thought she should come in by the 14th to remain in town. Eleanor dashed off a note to Betty who was waiting in Ottawa. We thought we had the situation licked.

The next few days Eleanor worked hard getting the room ready for Betty and trying to have the house on the top line. By the 7th we had more light snow and the temperature dropped to twenty below. I removed the battery from the jeep and placed it behind the stove in the kitchen to keep it alive. We listened to every weather forecast on the radio. On the 8th when I took the team and sleigh to see Angus it began to dawn on me that the by-pass around the dam as well as through the stubble field was just about impassable. But we could hope to pull the jeep through there with the horses. I kept the news from Eleanor.

Each day I had grown more apprehensive and hesitant to call on the neighbours for further assistance. The morning of the 9th, with five days to go, I remembered how Louis had figured to cross Tennessee Coulee by going north, and taking saddle horse I rode over our steepest hill east to look at the country from the top of the ridge. From there the country falls away sharply to farm land a few miles away and undulates gently to the valley where lies Pincher Creek. Thinking there might be a chance of climbing up to this ridge, I tested the cattle trail which leads down the other side to our east boundary fence and into the Neufeld ranch

234

where the graded road starts. Here also is the beginning of Tennessee Coulee, at this point only a small creek. The horse began to sink into the drift until I wondered if I was looking at the tops of bushes or trees. When the horse was shoulder deep and beginning to struggle I pulled him out. No way around at that point and the drift was a couple of hundred yards long. But if I could dig it out in a day the rest might be possible. By cutting around where no vehicle could go I rode across to the Neufeld buildings. Henry said they were keeping the road open and a jeep could get through with four chains. He offered his jeep if we had to get over there by sleigh and I told him we had to figure it out by the 14th, five days away. Riding back I checked the big drift again and decided digging it out was worth a try.

The weather was bright and warm on the 10th. No word from Betty yet. As the telephone line was out of order from the strong winds, we hoped there was a telegram waiting in Cowley. Little did we realize at this time that before we were through having our Porcupine Hill baby everyone would be in the act, that it would take teamwork of a high order to face such an emergency.

I kept the calves in the corral and after watering and feeding went up to the house. I told Eleanor I was riding over the hill to dig out the drift, that it would only take a few hours. I didn't tell her that on the flat and up the hill were twelve to fourteen inches of loose snow. Eleanor suggested a cup of coffee first and while I was warming up in the kitchen she went to the bedroom to lie down. Piles of dirty clothing were sorted out all over the kitchen floor, tubs of hot water waited on the stove. This was to be the last big wash and then Eleanor was going to clean the house once more before sitting back to wait. Betty was to find everything in order. All I had to do before leaving was to drink the coffee, start the little engine for the washing machine and leave Eleanor to it. That's what I thought.

There was a plaintive call from the bedroom. Would I go in there and leave the children in the kitchen? One minute I was young, determined and healthy. In the next ten minutes I was ageing far too quickly. Eleanor whispered in dismay that it was too late to get out. What were we going to do? I thought about jeeps and hills, snow and more snow, team and cold sleighs, the long miles between us and safety, the awful penalty of a wrong decision.

I tried to rush from one room to another, over and around piles of dirty clothing and little people always in the way, talking about the chance of getting somewhere in a couple of hours. Eleanor called out it was too late. If the telephone was working between here and town perhaps I could get hold of a woman. I made three local calls but everyone was out. I spoke to one woman but her man had gone to town with the team.

That did it. I turned back to Eleanor and told her we would just have to get over the hill to Neufeld's where there were three men and a housekeeper. I could make it in forty minutes. She would have a woman with her and a fighting chance of getting the doctor to come out.

"But what if we get stuck in the drift half way?"

I told her we wouldn't get stuck and hoped it sounded convincing.

"How about the children?"

I told her they would be better off over there.

Then she couldn't hold back the tears at the thought of Betty coming out to this confusion, with the laundry all over the place and the house not ready after all her planning.

But I wasn't thinking of these things. I was throwing clothes at Dane and Timmy, aged five and two, telling them to get into their snowsuits as best they could. I tried to help Eleanor get her things ready, rushed for the jeep, then remembered the battery behind the stove. Somehow I thought the time it would take to get team and sleigh would not compensate for an immediate start. If we did get stuck Henry could drive his jeep up to meet us and we would effect a transfer downhill. The battery went into place but the connections would not fit. In the panic of the moment I tied the loose one with binder twine, hammered the tight one on. She started. I backed out and put the kids in while the engine was warming up. Back in the house again I fetched Eleanor's suitcases and tried to find a spare garment for Timmy. Both boys looked like tramps, but this wasn't a social call. Eleanor still had misgivings about trying to leave but I managed to get her into the jeep. It wasn't a happy or carefree moment.

In four-wheel drive and tractor gear we started out. It wasn't encouraging to find we could barely crawl over the flat, pushing the snow up over the radiator, with chains on all four wheels, for there was a big climb ahead. We couldn't get on the grass slope to start the climb until we had backed and shovelled the deepest snow away. Once committed to the climb we had to give the little engine everything, but we struggled to the top. I had been reasonably certain we should get there but now we had to make the decision that would spell success or failure. Should we try our luck and roll down the steepest part of the descent, hoping the vehicle would remain on top of the deep drift?

If the jeep broke through and high-centred we would be pinned down for many hours. Time was the factor, so I decided against it, swung south on top of the ridge to keep going. Here the snow was not too deep and we picked our way through the evergreens, over hard little short drifts, around deadfall timber, over stumps and rocks, down a dip and up on to the ridge again. But we kept going. We worked south and east again until we were on an east-west ridge giving us a clear view south to our target. Directly below we could also see the Neufeld buildings. There was only one way down, a very steep vertical drop that in summer is marked by a single cattle trail. I remembered asking why this track was worn in such an impossible place for the brutes to climb and had been told that in the toughest winters it was the only way out of the pocket.

I left the jeep and walked part way down to look, noticing the heads of wild hay sticking through the snow, trying to judge the slope for 'sidling'. If the vehicle could only track straight down without slewing we might make it. But if she changed direction anywhere during the descent we could roll over and over . . . I had looked at this spot the other day when it was bare of snow and it reminded me of the landing hill below a ski jump.

I asked Eleanor if she was game to try, said it would be all over in a few minutes, then she would be safe in the house. She braced herself and said: "Let's go." I put the

238

jeep in low gear, told the kids in the back to hang on . . . and we crept over the lip.

When the little vehicle tipped forward the boys were thrown off their seats and remained piled up against the back of ours, howling their heads off. We held our breath. I talked to myself on the way down, hardly daring to use brakes and handling the wheel as gingerly as possible.

We made the bottom after an eternity, stopped to get our breath and right the kids. Then we broke out of the valley to Neufeld's and the open road. When I pulled up at the house Eleanor decided to remain where she was until I had telephoned the doctor. If the road report was still good she thought we might keep going. Henry followed in his jeep and we made the dash in record time. It took two and a half hours from start to finish and it was a real family affair with Tippy, our collie, managing to stay with us all the way to Pincher Station. At the hospital a very tired old man, who that morning had been young and reasonably gay, handed his wife over to the cool competence of the staff. The relief was temporary for I had two apprehensive children on my hands and a ranch full of livestock back in the hills.

It is funny the things a chap does between crises. I took the jeep to a garage for servicing. The mechanic was amused to find the battery in backward. The gauge had registered discharge all the way to town! I bought the boys some candy and then we wandered into Mr. Graham's barber shop. It seemed to be something to do until the next problem was solved, so Dane had a haircut and Timmy talked to lots of people.

Then the two little boys were left in the care of a very

239

kind couple we had met only recently. They offered to look after them until Betty should arrive. Now where was Betty? I telephoned to Cowley and learned that she would be arriving Saturday. This was Thursday. After a few hours of sleep I drove back to the ranch to look after the animals. Taking the same route I tried the steep slope in the same tracks while the Neufeld hands watched from a sleigh in the valley floor, betting on my chances. I figured if the jeep should stick I could back down and walk home, but she climbed steadily, like an old elevator.

I had assured Eleanor that I would do the washing somehow and put the finishing touches to the house. Just as I finished a meal and was deciding where to start in this domestic wilderness, Angus rode up on his sorrel. We moved furniture around and I swept the floor, moaning about the big wash. Angus decided he would come up with a sleigh and take it down to his wife. We threw all the neat little piles into one awful looking mound in the shed at the back.

The telephone began to work and I called Pincher Creek. Dr. Collins said Eleanor had presented the ranch with another cowboy. Both were fine. Holy cow! Another boy, and she had really wanted a girl! I opened a bottle of brandy. In our relief at the news Angus and I shook hands for a good five minutes. I began to telephone the neighbours asking if they wanted another hand. All the work waiting to be done around the house suddenly became very unimportant and I made plans to break out once again. Gus and his family were standing by and it didn't take long to arrange for son Marcel to come up here and take over. I don't remember this second trip, so it must have been made in a daze of thankfulness that all was well. Eleanor looked wonderful and the boy was a winner.

It seemed as if all our troubles were over. All I had to do was meet Betty next day, take her out to the ranch with the boys and relax while Eleanor had a good rest in hospital. It was a fitting climax after such an upset to our carefully laid plans. I thought of Robert Burns' 'The best laid schemes o' mice and men gang aft agley'. Plan how you might, you cannot force your will on weather, nature and their effect on railway time tables.

I'll never know just how our wonderful telephone operator at Cowley kept in touch with events. When I arrived at Pincher Station to meet Betty on Saturday there she was on the telephone, speaking from Lethbridge. She was stranded because her train had arrived four hours late and missed the connection. I told her to take a ten o'clock train that would arrive at midnight. Before that time a first-class blizzard struck the country—the daddy of all the winter storms. Her train was now expected at 3 a.m. Sunday. I crawled out from Pincher Creek to the station, a distance of two miles, with visibility sometimes nil, sometimes a few feet, reaching from one telephone pole to the next and stopping to determine if I was still on the road. Mine was the last vehicle to travel that road before the storm blew itself out. From 3.30 a.m. on, the station filled up with train crews looking like embattled warriors. The drifting snow, which quickly filled the jeep and hid it from view, was immobilizing the great mountain locomotives. Crews in relays kept trying to dig the engines out to get them started while the operator hugged the telegraph key. Betty's train arrived at 7.30 a.m., after engines had gone down to bring it up the grade by the Piegan Indian Reserve at Brocket. They had to split the train in two sections.

Mr. and Mrs. Bundy at the station had stayed up all night keeping the wires open and serving coffee and sandwiches to the crews. They took Betty into the fold. They were old hands at this sort of thing and to them it was a very natural thing to do. After a breakfast that raised our spirits they put me to bed. The blizzard persisted without slackening all Sunday; it wasn't until Monday noon that snow ploughs were able to open the two miles to Pincher Creek. I made the trip in a sleigh to get a wrecking truck for the jeep. Betty joined the children while I set out for the ranch.

There was no sign of the emergency route we had taken, but it kept luring me on like a challenge. I kept trying to find a way through the coulees, working north to the top of them, and got to within five miles of the Neufeld ranch before turning back. Driving to Cowley on the highway I traded the jeep for a team and got home at midnight with relays of horses. On Wednesday I returned to Cowley by sleigh and picked up the jeep. A snow plough had been out and we managed to get the children home by way of Neufeld's.

I wanted to settle down for a good long stretch of peaceful routine but by Sunday Eleanor was clamoring to be home. Why on earth couldn't she leave the hospital and visit in town until the weather improved? All winter she had been talking about the rest she was going to enjoy, the lazy life in town. But here she was just aching to be back on the ranch, whatever the weather. So I had to do the trip again over the hill east and that steep slope provided the same thrill. But three times without a crack-up was enough! With the baby along I wasn't going to tempt the fates again. We returned from Neufeld's in a sleigh, baby Ian, nine days old, having his first sleigh ride. The team couldn't pull the hill, and in attempting to traverse the sleigh nearly upset with two men hanging to the topside. Eleanor voted to get off and climb to the top on foot, carrying the baby. She wanted to get home in the worst way, and she did. With the driver and me hanging on to the sleigh we made the top but we wouldn't have tried it a second time on a bet.

We are all getting our youth back and I must say a family of five is pretty nice. The blizzards and snow and blocked roads are only a memory—something to talk about in later years. Life in the hills can dish up a mess of winter weather that hits with the fury of pent-up vengeance. Then spring comes and strokes the land with a gentle touch of magic. Everything turns green, melting snow swells the little streams, the water gurgles down from the heights. You awaken to a new world of buds, the cawing of crows, the bright flash of bluebirds. And you forgive nature for her pranks.

We are thankful to be back to normal again, but it's a busier normal. There is a little bundle of lovable, cooing humanity to share it with us. Dane and Timmy are fascinated.

And Eleanor? She's the same old gal, taking everything in her stride. During the winter she swore she wouldn't have time this year for a big garden or baby chicks but I didn't notice any difference when I sent off the seed order.

I knew she wouldn't be able to waste a single broody hen and I have caught her tucking turkey eggs under them when they weren't looking.

Just the other evening she said the baby bonus cheque is going to help a lot. It has been increased to fifteen whole dollars a month to be spent at her discretion.

"Why," she said brightly, "just think what I could do with twenty!"

ue